# AWESOME IDEAS

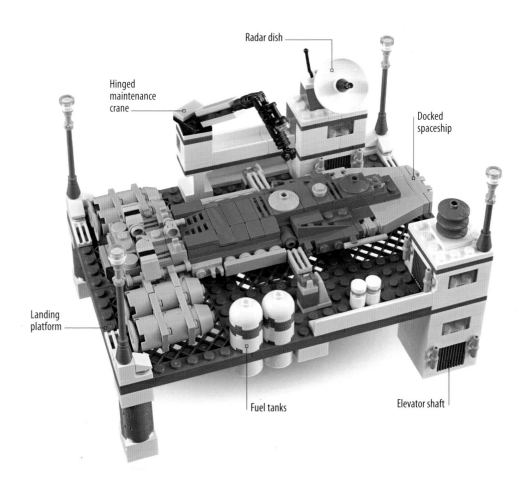

Radar dish

Hinged
maintenance
crane

Docked
spaceship

Landing
platform

Fuel tanks

Elevator shaft

LEGO® Technic right angle axle connector

2x2 brick

Flame

1x4 brick with side studs

Loudhailer

2x2 round brick

1x2 inverted slope

1x2 printed tile

4x4 car roof

Steering wheel

1x2 grille slope

2x2 plate with double wheels

Globe

Telescope

Pig

Propeller with 3 blades

Mailbox with door

1x2 curved half arch

1x1 headlight brick

1x12x3 arch

1x2 brick

Seat with 2x2 base

Bush

LEGO Technic cross axle

Flower

1x3 curved slope

2x3 slope

2x2 printed round tile

Hinge plates

Train buffers

1x2 grille

# AWESOME
# IDEAS

Smokestack

Roof

Engine cover

Roof supports

Driver

Cowcatcher

Train wheels

**DANIEL LIPKOWITZ**

# Contents

# Book breakdown

This book shows lots of inspiring model breakdowns to help you discover ideas and techniques for your own models, but the entire book is broken down, too. There are many different types of pages designed to help you build up your own amazing LEGO® world, section by section, model by model, brick by brick.

Colored bars, like the one below, run along the top of pages to let you know what kind of page you're reading.

Page number | Section name

10    OUTER SPACE     ROBOTS     How to build

Chapter name | Page type

Here are all the different types of pages you'll find in this book:

## How to build
Watch one model develop from start to finish on these pages, with helpful building advice at every stage.

## What else can you build?
Once you've seen how to build one model, discover different ways of using similar techniques and ideas in your own models.

## Model galleries
Little details can really help build up a scene. Check out these pages for a collection of smaller models you can make using a small number of bricks.

## Expanding your world
Don't stop now! Once you've built a few models, why not add more to your world? These pages give ideas for building extra models and scenery.

## Builder secrets
Ssshh! These pages reveal insider tips for building challenging parts of models or functions. Master the techniques to wow your friends!

## Showstoppers
These pages show off the biggest or most interesting ideas in this book. Look at them in detail and use the ideas to build your own showstopper models.

## Dioramas
On these pages, see most of the models in a chapter in one awesome scene.

LETS GET STARTED!

# What every builder needs to know...

A great LEGO® model starts with an imaginative idea, but it also requires some technical know-how. These useful notes for builders explain some of the terms and techniques you'll find throughout this book.

## Vocabulary

It may sound like LEGO builders are speaking their own secret language, but once you've learned a few key phrases you can sound like a pro, too.

### Stud

The round raised bumps on top of bricks and plates are called studs. Studs fit perfectly into "tubes", which are on the bottom of bricks and plates.

### Brick

Bricks form the basis of most models. They come in a variety of shapes, sizes, colors, and textures to suit whatever it is you want to create.

### Plate

A plate is very similar to a brick, as it has studs on top and tubes underneath. The key difference is that a plate is much thinner than a brick.

### Tile

A tile is thin like a plate, but flat on top. Try using them to give your build a smooth surface, either for decoration or to make a smooth base for sliding parts.

### Hole

Bricks and plates with holes are helpful if you want to join parts of your model together. Holes can hold connecting pieces like bars, axles, and LEGO® Technic pins.

## Geometry

1x2, 6x6, 1x2x6... sometimes talking about LEGO pieces might seem like being in a math lesson. The geometry behind LEGO measurements is actually really simple once you've got the hang of it.

### Measurements

Builders often describe the size of LEGO pieces according to the number of studs on them. If a brick has 2 studs across and 3 up, it's a 2x3 brick. A 4x4 round plate is named because it is 4 studs across at its widest points.

← 2 →

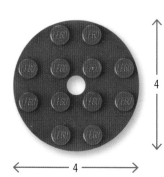
← 4 →

3
← 1 →

4

3

### Brick height

If a piece name has three numbers, the third number relates to its height. Height is measured in the size of standard bricks. For example, a 1x2x5 brick is 5 times taller than a normal 1x2 brick.

### Plate height

One brick is exactly the same height as 3 plates stacked together. This means it would take 15 plates to reach the same height as the 1x2x5 brick!

Five stacked 1x2 bricks

=

1x2x5 brick

1x2 brick

=

Three stacked 1x2 plates

*SINCE I DON'T HAVE HAIR, I'M EXACTLY FOUR BRICKS HIGH.*

### Area

When you start building a model it is good to start with a baseplate and build up. The largest baseplate the LEGO Group makes is 48x48 studs, but if you only have smaller plates don't worry! If you need an 8x16 base, try using two 8x8 plates, or four 4x8 plates. You can join these together with small plates or bricks on top as you begin to build.

8x16 plate   =

Two 8x8 plates   =   +

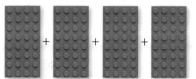
Four 4x8 plates
+   +   +

# Ways to build

There are many different ways to put your LEGO pieces together. Some help make your model more stable, some make it look prettier and some make it move.

## Upward

A simple stack of bricks is useful for building thin columns and adding stripes of color, but staggering bricks in a LEGO wall makes it stronger, just like bricks in a real-life brick wall!

Stacked bricks

Staggered bricks

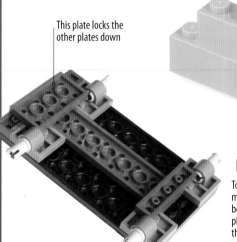

This plate locks the other plates down

## Downward

To secure the base of your model, try overlapping the bottom pieces with sturdy plates underneath. These lock the top pieces together to make an extra strong connection.

## Sideways

If you want to add detail to the sides of your creations, build using pieces that have studs on the sides. Pieces can then be attached to a build sideways. LEGO builders call this technique Studs Not On Top, or SNOT.

1x1 brick with studs on 4 sides

## All around

Add interesting angles or moving parts to your models using hinges or joints. These come in a variety of different forms, each one giving a different type of movement or shape to your model.

Hinge plates

1x2 hinge brick and 2x2 hinge plate

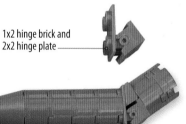

# Scale

Before you begin building, think carefully about how big you want your model to be. This can depend on the number of bricks you have, how long you have to build, or how you want to play with your model when its finished. Here are the three main scales builders might build in.

*HOORAY! THIS CAR IS JUST RIGHT!*

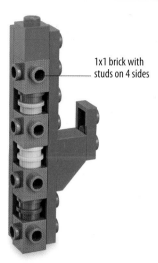

## Minifigure scale

Most of the models in this book are built in the scale of a LEGO minifigure. Building at this scale means your minifigures can live in and drive your models.

*THIS SHIP IS TOO SMALL!*

*THIS COMB IS TOO BIG!*

## Micro-scale

This scale is useful for building models that appear to be in the distance. You could create an entire space battle with tiny spaceships like this one, but you have to imagine the tiny passengers!

## Real size

Sometimes, it's fun to build something fit for humans instead of for minifigures. This size works well for real-life objects, such as a LEGO comb.

# OUTER SPACE

The year is 2531. The deep-space starship *Zycon* has arrived in orbit above the small, uncharted world of Volga. The intrepid crew's task is to land on the planet's surface, study its scientific properties, and build a new research colony here. Who knows what encounters or discoveries they will have on their expedition, but one thing is certain: they're going to need a whole lot of bricks!

# A mech walker

Touchdown! The astronauts have landed and their first objective is to build something to help them survey this unknown world. The planet Volga's landscape is rocky and uneven, so feet will work better than wheels. The colony is going to need a mech walker.

**START HERE**

Ball-joint pieces from a LEGO® Hero Factory or LEGO® BIONICLE® set

Armor piece snaps onto the ball in the upper leg

A high front blocks the ankle from bending too far forward

## 1  Feet first

Start by building the mech's legs and feet. Hinges are good for making moving limbs, but ball joints will give you the most flexibility. A big, chunky foot helps to make your mech stable.

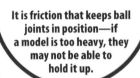

It is friction that keeps ball joints in position—if a model is too heavy, they may not be able to hold it up.

You'll need a heavy back end to balance this long nose

Bricks with built-in sockets connect the ball joints at the tops of the legs

Transparent light blue elements create a glowing effect

Plates with side rings are great attachment points for equipment

## 2  Cockpit base

While a robot moves on its own, a mech needs a pilot. Create the base for a cockpit by attaching the legs to a plate big enough for a seated minifigure pilot.

Inverted slopes bulk up the underside of the cockpit

*I CAN'T WAIT TO STOMP AROUND MY NEW PLANET.*

## 3  Sturdy body

Add pieces to build up the mech's main body, taking care to leave room for the pilot. This is a good time to start adding lights and other robotic details.

**REAR VIEW**

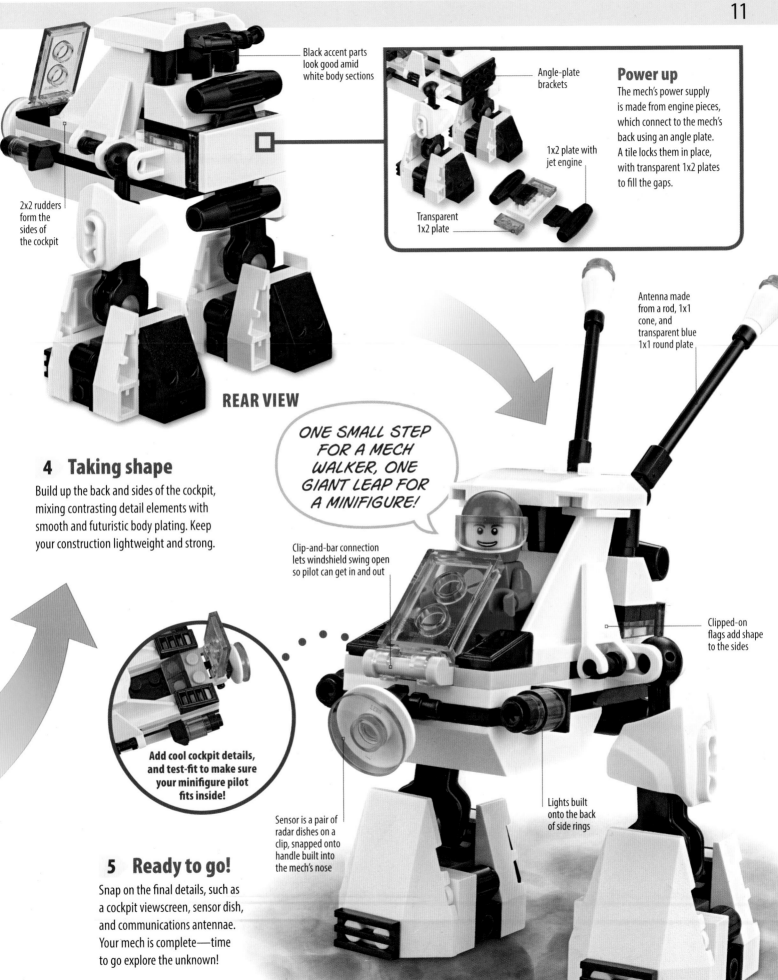

Black accent parts look good amid white body sections

2x2 rudders form the sides of the cockpit

Angle-plate brackets

**Power up**
The mech's power supply is made from engine pieces, which connect to the mech's back using an angle plate. A tile locks them in place, with transparent 1x2 plates to fill the gaps.

1x2 plate with jet engine

Transparent 1x2 plate

**REAR VIEW**

Antenna made from a rod, 1x1 cone, and transparent blue 1x1 round plate

ONE SMALL STEP FOR A MECH WALKER, ONE GIANT LEAP FOR A MINIFIGURE!

#### 4 Taking shape
Build up the back and sides of the cockpit, mixing contrasting detail elements with smooth and futuristic body plating. Keep your construction lightweight and strong.

Clip-and-bar connection lets windshield swing open so pilot can get in and out

Clipped-on flags add shape to the sides

**Add cool cockpit details, and test-fit to make sure your minifigure pilot fits inside!**

Lights built onto the back of side rings

Sensor is a pair of radar dishes on a clip, snapped onto handle built into the mech's nose

#### 5 Ready to go!
Snap on the final details, such as a cockpit viewscreen, sensor dish, and communications antennae. Your mech is complete—time to go explore the unknown!

# All-purpose robots

Thanks to the mech walker's recon work, the astronauts have chosen a location for their new space colony. To aid them during its construction, they assemble a group of helpful mini-robots, each with its own special programming and function.

**WHAT'S NEXT?**

**CAMERA-BOTS**

A mech has to be big enough to carry a pilot around in, but when building a robot, you can make it as big or as small as you want.

**COMMAND-BOT**

Body connects to legs using a plate with a ring, making the bot posable

*ARE YOU MY ROBOT BROTHER?*

Legs are minifigure revolvers

Radar dish foot

## Camera-bots

You only need a handful of small pieces to make a robot. These ones have sophisticated camera eyes that keep watch for natural hazards and alien life-forms.

*NO, I'M YOUR TRANSISTOR.*

Use a 1x2 plate with a vertical bar to attach weapons or tools

Walkie-talkie for communicating with other robots

## Command-bot

With its long, swiveling arms, this command-bot can perform basic scientific experiments and emergency first aid. Since the command-bot's role doesn't require it to go very far, it has no legs!

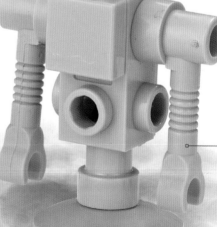

*GET BACK TO WORK, YOU! (BEEP)*

Swiveling arms made from wrench pieces

If you want your robot to move around, this radar dish can be a hover-booster

## MAINTENANCE-BOT

### Maintenance-bot

This more advanced robot works on the crew's shuttle in partnership with a forklift robot (pages 14–15). By using lots of small pieces, you can build robots with interesting extra details and plenty of personality.

1x1 plate with clip hands hold minifigure tools

### Moving parts

The maintenance-bot's head and limbs are attached to its body with clip-and-bar connections, giving them movement. A bar holder with clip for the neck lets the bot's head swing up and down and from side-to-side.

Legs attach to 1x1 bricks with handled bars

Slopes and curves fill out the body shape

Big feet keep the bot from falling over

## WORKER-BOT

## GUARD-BOT

### Worker-bot

This tough, compact robot is a mechanical jack-of-all-trades designed to help in assembly and repair work. Built-in pistons give it impressive strength for its size.

Claws fit into wrists of robot arm elements

Double-barreled blasters create piston details

Zapper-pole made from a bar, lightsaber handle, and transparent 1x1 bulb

Claws act like clips for holding bar-shaped objects

### Guard-bot

This armored robot defends the exterior of the base. Clip-and-bar connections make its limbs posable, and its gripper claws let it carry a defensive zapper-pole.

Legs are the same pieces as the hand-claws

Feet are 1x2 plates with bars, with tiles on top

### Tele-shoulders

The guard-bot's head is connected to its body with telephone handsets. Its robot arm shoulders clip onto the middle part of the handset.

# Forklift robot

This all-terrain forklift robot transports cargo that is too heavy for the astronauts to carry. Combine parts and features from rolling vehicles and walking mechs to build a robot with multiple modes.

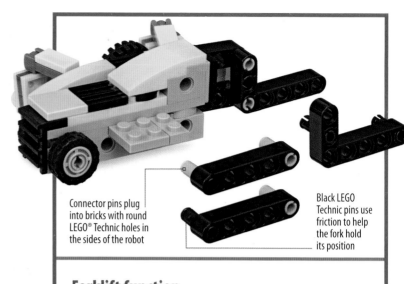

Connector pins plug into bricks with round LEGO® Technic holes in the sides of the robot

Black LEGO Technic pins use friction to help the fork hold its position

### Forklift function

The forklift mechanism is made using four LEGO Technic half beams, two 7-hole L-shaped beams, and a mix of friction and free-spinning LEGO Technic connector pins.

## On the move

The forklift robot uses its heavy-treaded wheels to roll across smooth planetary landscapes. When the ground becomes rough and uneven, it deploys its four ball-jointed limbs and walks the rest of the way.

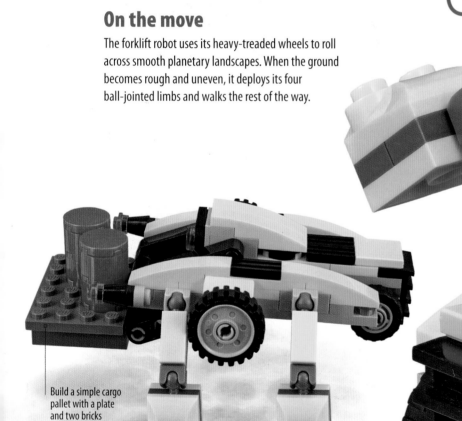

Leg design influenced by insect limbs

Build a simple cargo pallet with a plate and two bricks

**WALKING MODE**

Ladder in back lets astronauts climb aboard

## Lift off

When making a LEGO model with a moving function, try building the function first. Once it works the way you want it to, then you can design the rest of the model around it.

**FORKLIFT IN LOWERED POSITION**

Cargo containers are made with two 2x2 round bricks and a 2x2 round tile on top

Parallel beams above and below keep the fork level when it moves up and down

**FORKLIFT IN RAISED POSITION**

Forward light is a 1x1 cone and round plate attached to a plate with side ring

These small ball-joint elements are found in many LEGO creature sets

Legs retracted for rolling mode

*HEY! WATCH WHERE YOU'RE PUTTING YOUR EXTRA LEGS.*

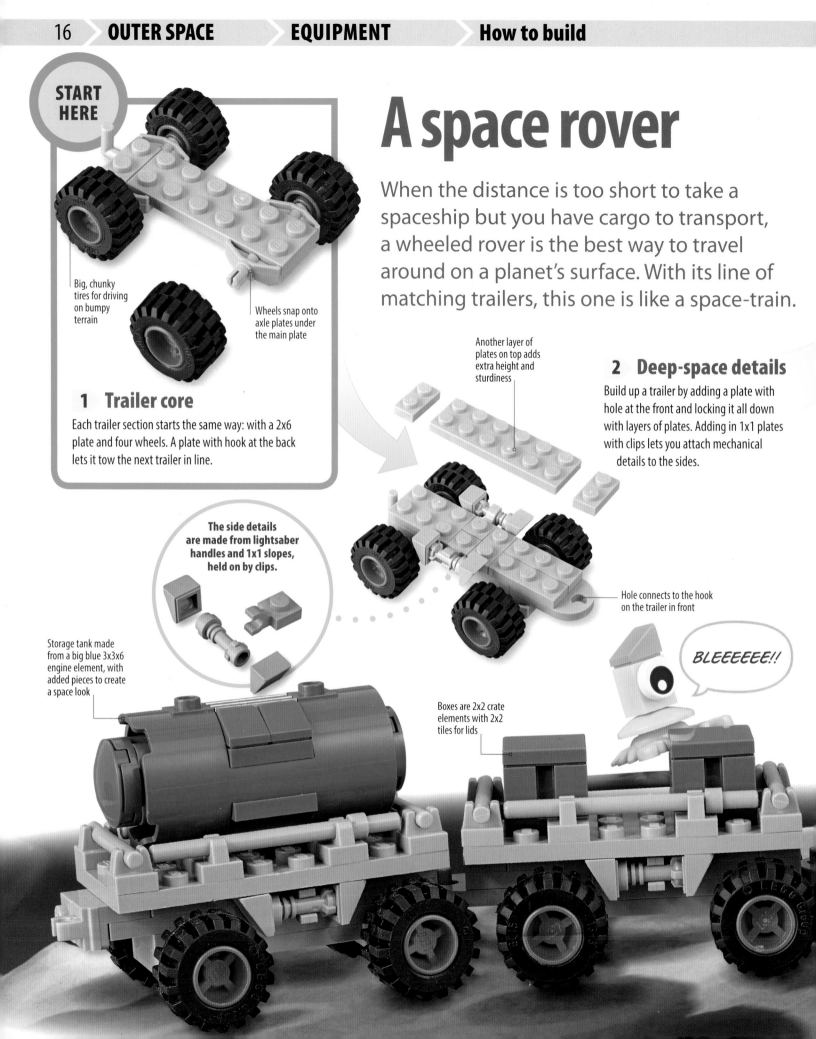

**START HERE**

Big, chunky tires for driving on bumpy terrain

Wheels snap onto axle plates under the main plate

# A space rover

When the distance is too short to take a spaceship but you have cargo to transport, a wheeled rover is the best way to travel around on a planet's surface. With its line of matching trailers, this one is like a space-train.

Another layer of plates on top adds extra height and sturdiness

## 1 Trailer core

Each trailer section starts the same way: with a 2x6 plate and four wheels. A plate with hook at the back lets it tow the next trailer in line.

## 2 Deep-space details

Build up a trailer by adding a plate with hole at the front and locking it all down with layers of plates. Adding in 1x1 plates with clips lets you attach mechanical details to the sides.

The side details are made from lightsaber handles and 1x1 slopes, held on by clips.

Hole connects to the hook on the trailer in front

Storage tank made from a big blue 3x3x6 engine element, with added pieces to create a space look

Boxes are 2x2 crate elements with 2x2 tiles for lids

BLEEEEEE!!

1x2 jumper plates will hold a centered mini-build like the blue tank (see opposite page)

1x1 plate with top clip

If you don't have this 4x8 plate, build a similar shape out of multiple smaller plates

## 3  Secure platform

Attach a bigger plate as a flat platform for transporting equipment. Clips and bar pieces around the edge will keep the cargo from tumbling out if you hit a crater.

## 4  Ready to roll

What will this trailer be hauling? Attach jumper plates, tiles, clips, turntables, or any other pieces that will safely hold your equipment in place during the bumpy drive to the expedition's remote research outposts.

CAN'T PARK HERE. THERE'S A PARKING METEOR.

## Driver details

The driver carriage of the rover is built like a trailer, with some extra details added. Its headlights are built from two 1x1 plates with top clips, which attach to the sideways studs of an angle plate. Snap on a bar, then add two more plates with top clips with transparent 1x1 round plates for the lights.

Minifigure binoculars

Side rails plug into 1x1 bricks with hollow side studs

Angled front made with a tile on top of a snap-together hinge

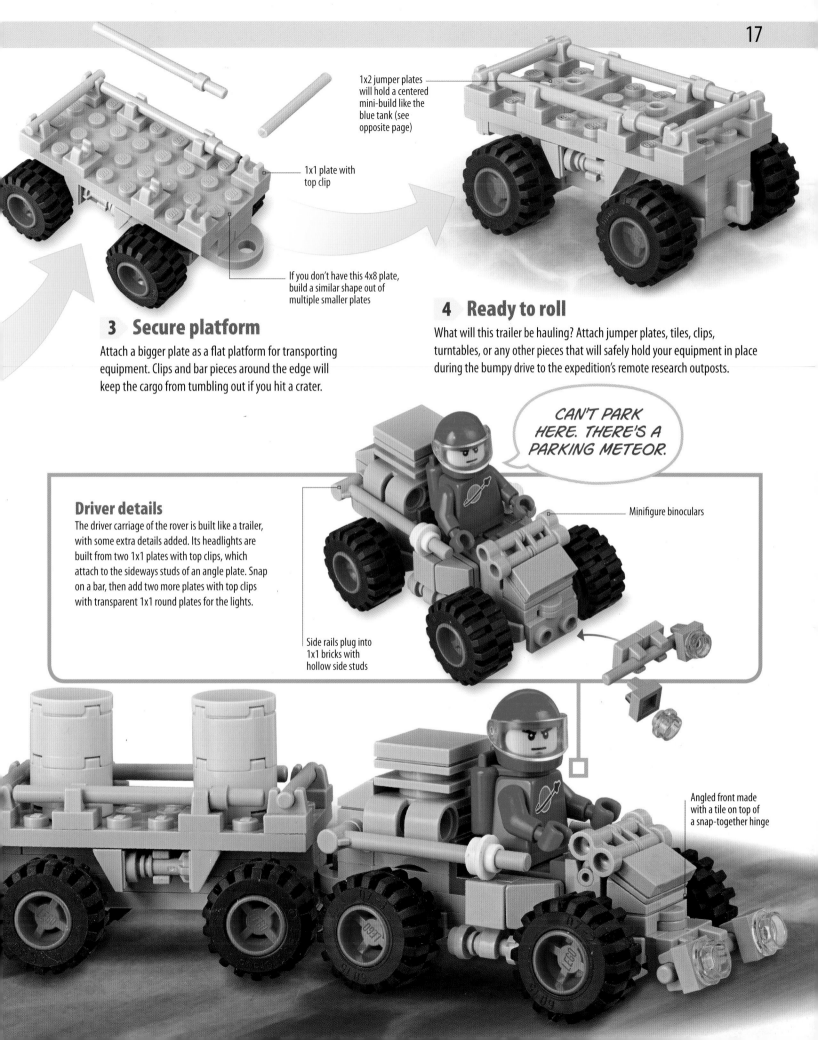

# Space equipment

It takes a lot of technology to live and work on a new planet. A skilled engineering crew is in charge of building all of the space-age equipment that the astronauts will need on the planet Volga.

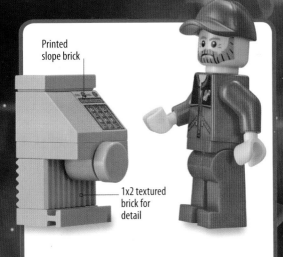

Printed slope brick

1x2 textured brick for detail

## Data console

Combine blocky and round elements to make a computer system that would be equally useful aboard a star cruiser or on an alien world.

Flexible tubes attached with clips for power cables

8x8 radar dish— or use the largest one you've got!

A clip-hinge connection lets the satellite dish pivot up and down.

Space trolley

Even astronauts have to push things around by hand sometimes. With its robotic arms to clamp cargo in place, this hi-tech handcart is reinforced for the most high-gravity planets.

Swiveling robot arms clip onto bars

Tire-less wheel hubs attached with LEGO Technic pins

A single-piece girder is stronger than a tall, thin tower built from multiple parts

## Satellite dish

A satellite installation on the planet's surface lets the expedition team communicate with their ship in orbit. Useful pieces here are a tall support girder and a big radar dish.

*ALL THIS ENERGY, JUST TO CHARGE MY PHONE.*

Panels made from transparent gray bricks, with transparent blue plates on top and below

Front bumper is a
single grille piece

Headlight clips onto
a bar piece attached to
the main body of the bike

Flag pieces attached to plates
with handled bars create
wings for flight stability

## Jet bike

A popular form of transport on frontier worlds, a jet bike is easy
to fly and fast. The main body of this one is built around a 2x4
plate base, with lots of side-stud bricks and pieces with clips
and bars that form attachment points for interesting details.

Engine exhausts made
from ray-gun pieces

## Generator

There's no need to carry spare batteries
halfway across the universe when
you've got a portable micro-fusion
generator. Small, unusually
shaped elements provide
the details.

Pipes and tubes
made with grilles,
revolvers, and
binoculars

An all-gray color scheme looks
functional and industrial

## Greebling

1x4 plates lock the hinges
together, while the revolvers
are held on by 1x1 plates with
top clips. Small mechanical
details like these are
referred to by LEGO
fans as "greebles."

Fuel cells built from two 2x2
round bricks, a 2x2 round
plate, and a 2x2 dome

## Energy array

Use flexible hoses to link several space modules
together into one multi-piece array, like a set of
solar panels, a fuel cell replenishment platform,
and a spinning wind turbine.

Build a broad
solid base, or just
use a base plate

# Planetary pod

While the colony is under construction, the astronauts stay inside this temporary habitation module. Dropped onto the planet from orbit, it may be a little cramped, but it has everything that the crew needs to survive on an alien world.

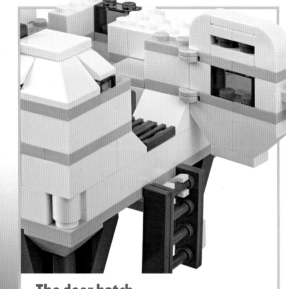

### The door hatch

The hatch is constructed almost exactly the same way as the windows (opposite), but with hinge plates to let it swing open, and a 1x1 brick with vertical bar for a grip.

Articulated armature made from LEGO Technic T-bars and robot arms

Removable roof built on an 8x8 plate

Roof-corner slope

### Space house

The pod is built as a basic square shape, but slopes and detail pieces keep it from just being a simple box. Stilt-like legs raise it off the ground, and a ladder leads up to the opening airlock hatch. A communications dish on top lets it stay in contact with the colony ship.

Support legs made from inverted slopes, 1x1 round bricks, and L-shaped corner bricks at the bottom

Build in transparent pieces (like these 1x1 plates) for glowing lights

Ladder is a 1x4 barred fence with a tile covering its studs, attached to the module by a 1x2 plate with clips

# Home sweet module

The square roof rests on the corners of four 2x2 tiles on top of the module. When its removed, a small living area is revealed inside. It has twin reclining beds, a work desk with a recessed computer station, a food preparation area, and a cupboard for storing space-exploration gear.

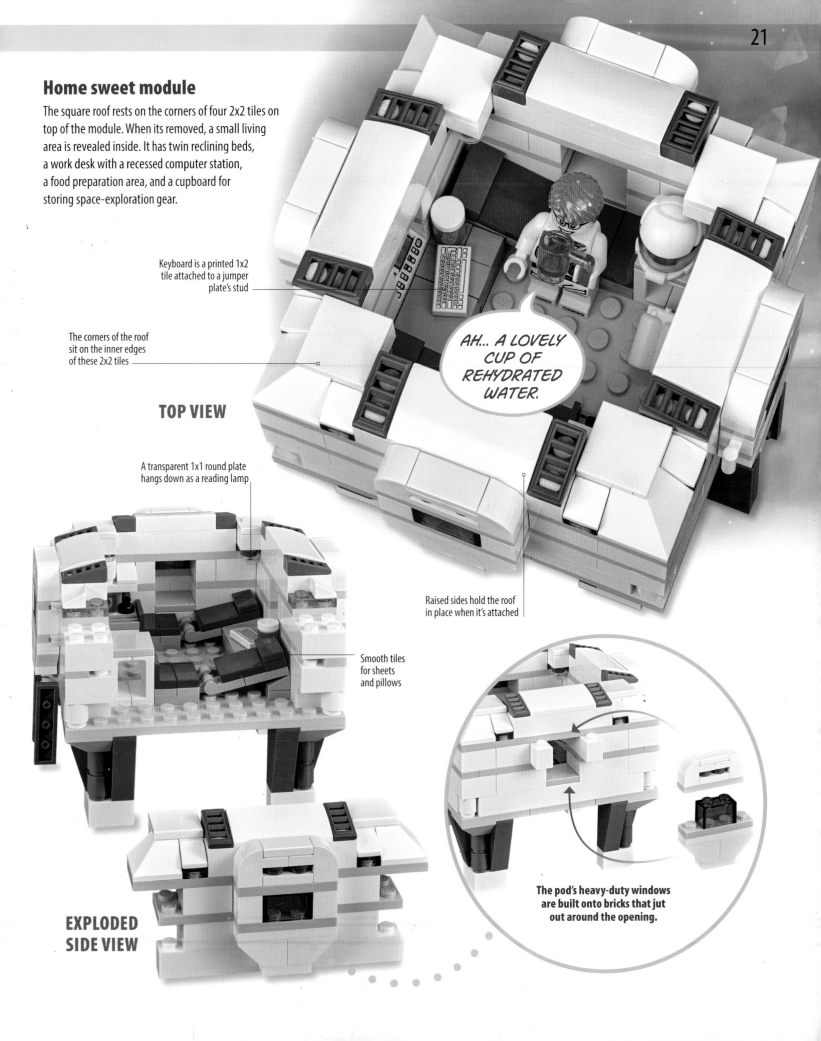

Keyboard is a printed 1x2 tile attached to a jumper plate's stud

The corners of the roof sit on the inner edges of these 2x2 tiles

**TOP VIEW**

*AH... A LOVELY CUP OF REHYDRATED WATER.*

A transparent 1x1 round plate hangs down as a reading lamp

Raised sides hold the roof in place when it's attached

Smooth tiles for sheets and pillows

**EXPLODED SIDE VIEW**

**The pod's heavy-duty windows are built onto bricks that jut out around the opening.**

# A space door

New orders have arrived from the mission commander: it's time to start building the colony's workspaces. First, the crew must assemble a secure door to keep breathable air inside and space dust out.

**START HERE**

6x8 plate, or use several smaller plates side-by-side

Use plates with bars for a clip-and-bar hinge

## 1  Build the door

Start your model with the door itself. Think about how you want it to attach and open, and add extra pieces for detail and depth.

## 2  Wall base

Next, take a base plate and start building a wall. Leave a gap for a doorway that will be slightly smaller than the door, so that the door will stop against it when it's closed.

Use grilles for gratings and panels

Two-plate-high raised ledge keeps the door from swinging into the gap

**Try building a basic wall first to measure the size of the hole for the door.**

A tile locks the clip plate down

## 3  Door connections

Build clips for the door hinge into the wall. Be creative, but make sure they're attached firmly. This door's clip sections attach to 1x4 bricks with side studs built into the wall.

Ladder piece is a cooling vent

When the door is clipped in place, its top should be higher than this row of bricks

Build a matching wall on this side, but without the clips

## 4  Build it up

Build up the sides of the wall to make a frame for the doorway, adding in some blocky, sci-fi details to make your door unique. Keep this section a little shorter than the door itself.

Thicker sections add stability to the bottom of the wall

If you don't have pieces long enough to go all the way across, make staggered layers for sturdiness

Plates with side rails create a projecting lip above the door—perhaps it catches acidic space-rain!

## 5 Close the gap

With both sides built up to the same height, lay long plates or bricks across the entire wall to lock everything together and complete the top of the doorway.

The door should cover the entire hole and not fall off when you move it

This could be the inside or the outside of your colony

*LOVELY WEATHER FOR A SPACE-STROLL!*

## 6 Take a walk

Make a row of space-style details to go across the top and your space door is finished! Now your astronauts can safely enter and leave the colony. Use the same build with different colors and details to make other doors.

You could decorate the base plate with space station or alien terrain features

# Sci-fi doors and walls

Most doors are rectangles, and most walls are flat and smooth…but when you're imagining the future, your options are as infinite as the universe itself. Try some of these sci-fi builds for inspiration.

## Simple wall

An easy trick for walls is to make them out of large plates and attach them to a base using click hinges. Don't build them too high, or the hinges might not be strong enough to hold them up.

**SIMPLE WALL**

**PLATFORM SECTION**

**WHAT'S NEXT?**

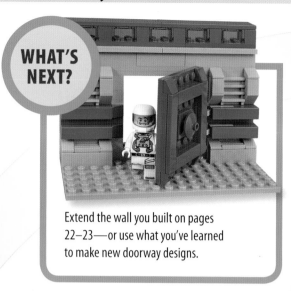

Extend the wall you built on pages 22–23—or use what you've learned to make new doorway designs.

Plates with gratings make great sci-fi wall panels

Blue and transparent yellow pattern echoes the design above the door without copying it exactly

Round tiles cover the studs in the center

These blue tiles continue the striped pattern of the space door section

This middle section is the door from the previous page

*WHAT'S IT LIKE OUT?*

*NOT MUCH ATMOSPHERE.*

Click-hinge connection

# SLIDING DOOR

**Hi-tech columns made with poles and 1x1 cones**

## Wide slide
The doors are built like mini-walls inside the box-like wall. Tiles underneath let them slide back and forth without sticking to the floor.

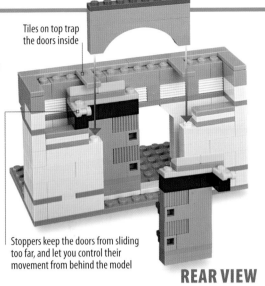

**Tiles on top trap the doors inside**

**Stoppers keep the doors from sliding too far, and let you control their movement from behind the model**

**REAR VIEW**

## Sliding doors
For a fun challenge with a real sci-fi flair, try building doors that slide open and closed. Make the wall around them extra thick, with a hollow space inside to hide the doors when they're open.

**Door handles are bars held by clips attached to 1x1 side-stud bricks**

**This could be an activation button or an emergency alert light**

## Futuristic flooring
The floor pattern is made by building a hollow space into the base. A wall of bricks made from textured pieces, tiles, and plates fits sideways into that space.

**Ladders alternate with slope bricks**

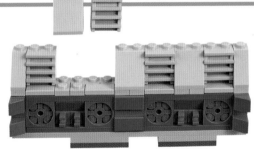

**Plates and tiles make the thin yellow stripe**

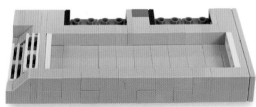

THAT DOOR STOP LOOKS SUSPICIOUS.

**Yellow grilles for high-visibility steps**

## Platform section
This section uses a much more advanced design than the simple wall opposite. Instead of a base plate, the floor is built out of bricks turned on their side. Sideways-building elements are used to attach a wall covered with detail pieces.

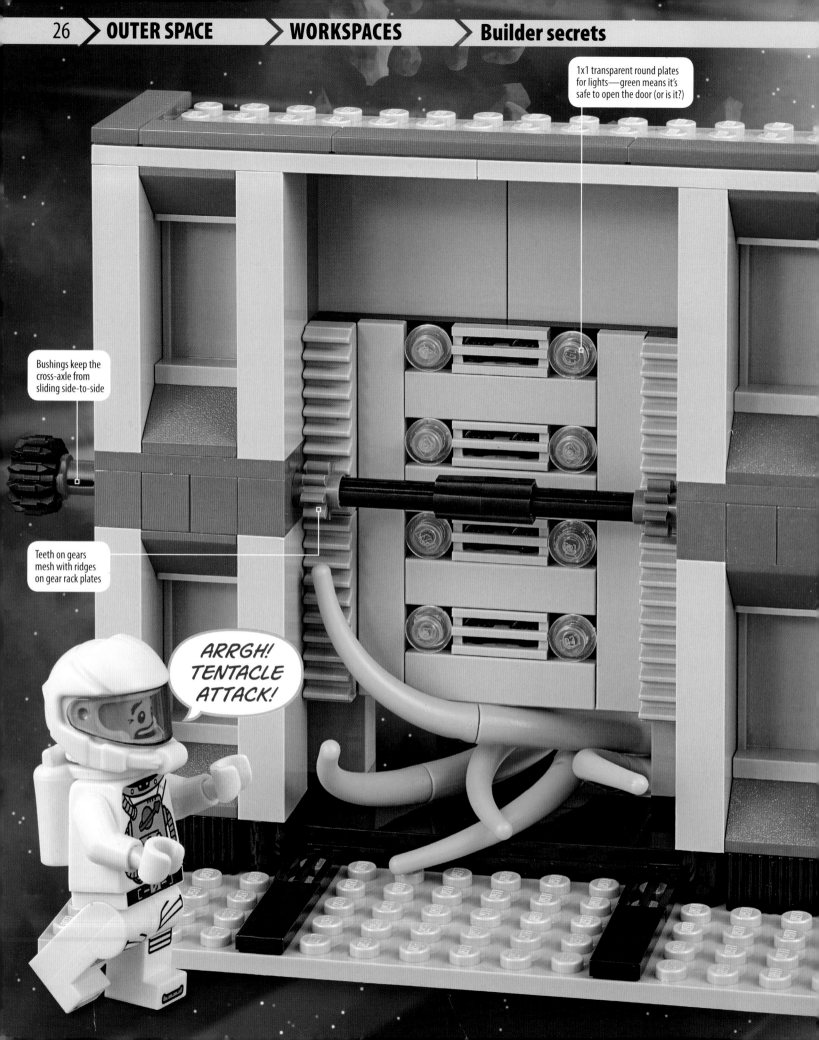

# Gear doorway

There are strange signals coming from outside this space doorway... The door uses LEGO Technic gears to make it rise at the turn of a knob—just watch out for who or what you're letting inside!

Line up bricks with holes so that the axle passes through them all

**The axle passes through a 1x4 brick with three round LEGO Technic holes.**

### 1  Holes in the wall

The door function requires a straight axle to pass all the way through the model from one side to the other. Build a doorway that contains bricks with round holes that will support the axle and let it rotate freely.

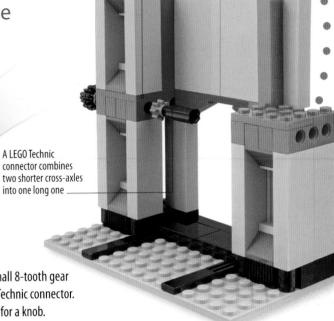

A LEGO Technic connector combines two shorter cross-axles into one long one

### 2  Add the axles

Slide cross axles through the holes in each side, placing a small 8-tooth gear on the inside. Join the two axles in the middle with a LEGO Technic connector. Push a bushing onto the outside end, and add another gear for a knob.

8-tooth gear

LEGO Technic cross-axle

Bushing

12-tooth double-bevel gear

**Make the door taller than the height of the gears so it doesn't fall out when closed.**

### 3  Drop in the door

Build a door and slide it into the mechanism from above, so that the 8-tooth gears on the cross-axles interlock with the gear rack plates on the door.

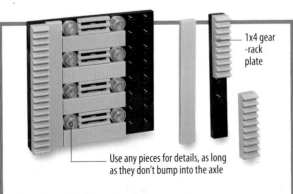

1x4 gear-rack plate

Use any pieces for details, as long as they don't bump into the axle

### Perfect fit

The key to this door's function is the width of the gear-rack plates on its outside edges. They are built on top of two plate layers, so that they fit snugly into the gears on the axles.

# Research lab

In the space colony's research laboratory, the science team studies samples from the planet in order to learn about living in their new home. This scientific workshop is full of futuristic instruments and hi-tech devices.

This fume hood sucks up toxic fumes and space germs

Open wall elements are lightweight but strong

TESTS SHOW THESE CARROTS ARE A LITTLE SMALL.

## Weird science

Here at the lab, technicians analyze minerals, atmospheric gases, and strange alien plants brought back by the survey crew. They have everything they need, from a fume hood for hazardous chemicals to a conveyor belt that carries items through a line of probes and scanners.

OPEN SESAME!

1x1 bricks with bars create door handles

Doors lead to other areas of the colony

## Laboratory doors

The laboratory's sliding doors are built similarly to the ones on page 25, but now they are incorporated into an entire room model.

This thick wall conceals the sliding doors when they're open

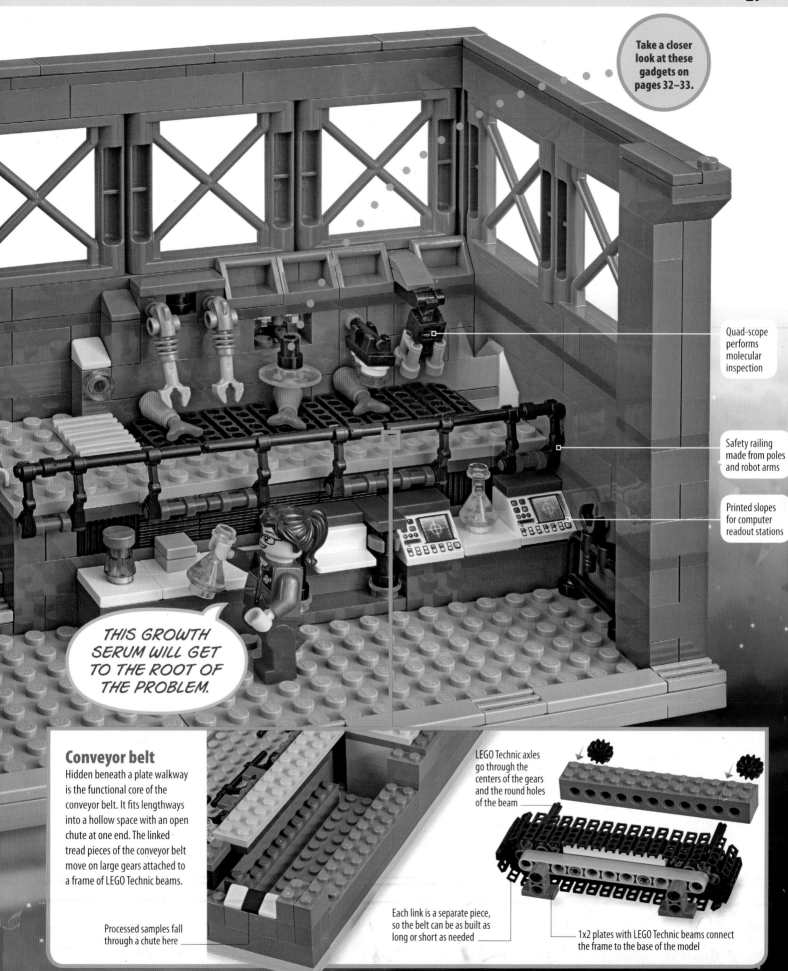

Take a closer look at these gadgets on pages 32–33.

Quad-scope performs molecular inspection

Safety railing made from poles and robot arms

Printed slopes for computer readout stations

THIS GROWTH SERUM WILL GET TO THE ROOT OF THE PROBLEM.

## Conveyor belt

Hidden beneath a plate walkway is the functional core of the conveyor belt. It fits lengthways into a hollow space with an open chute at one end. The linked tread pieces of the conveyor belt move on large gears attached to a frame of LEGO Technic beams.

LEGO Technic axles go through the centers of the gears and the round holes of the beam

Processed samples fall through a chute here

Each link is a separate piece, so the belt can be as built as long or short as needed

1x2 plates with LEGO Technic beams connect the frame to the base of the model

# Hydroponics bay

The hydroponics bay provides a temperature-controlled, nutrient-rich environment for growing edible plants. You could build this model on its own, or combine it with other colony modules such as the research lab.

## Space greenhouse

The space colony scientists won't go hungry on their new planet! They are growing their own food in abundance inside this hydroponics bay. Water tubes built into the walls of the chamber keep plants hydrated, and plants are "fed" through an elevated nutrient tank.

Carrots suspended inside a fast-growing growth tank (see more of this model on pages 32–33)

Water-carrying pipework made from telescopes and 1x1 round plates

WHAT DID PEOPLE EAT BEFORE WE HAD PIZZA-FRUIT?

Plant growth vitamins

These plants are stacks of three-leafed 1x1 elements, with 1x2 plates for fruit-bearing branches

Transparent blue plates for pools of water

This wheel controls the water pressure in the pipes

Looks like this fruit isn't ripe yet!

LEGO Technic connector pins attach the nutrient tank to a pair of LEGO Technic beams. The beams are snapped onto 2x2 bricks with side pins built into the top of the wall.

**SIDE VIEW**

The blue core of these clear tubes looks like flowing water

Nutrient tank is a two-piece cylinder from a LEGO Hero Factory set

## Connecting modules

You can place your modules side-by-side to connect up your research colony. Alternatively, a tile lining on top of the modules with a few exposed studs allows you to stack another colony module on top and then remove it easily.

# Lab tools gallery

Combine pieces with interesting shapes in new ways to invent the scientific tools of tomorrow. Use ray guns, binoculars, telescopes, faucets, robot arms, claws, radar dishes, and much more!

**FROG**

**SPACE CARROT**

**CHEMICAL FLASK**

**JAR**

**MECHANICAL CLAW**

**QUAD-SCOPE**

**MINI TOOL-RACK**

TIME FOR A DEEP SPACE CLEAN.

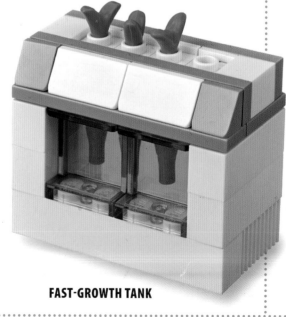

**FAST-GROWTH TANK**

**STERILIZER**

**WATER BUCKET**

**COLLECTION BOTTLE**

**FISH SPECIMEN**

**ATOMIZER**

**SPECTRUM DISH**

**WATER TANK**

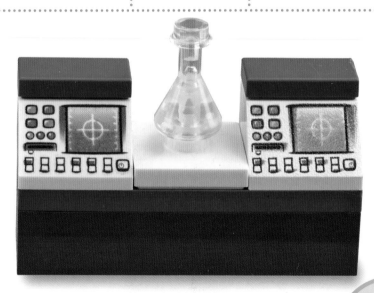

**READOUT STATION**

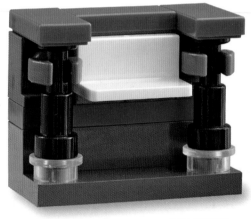

**LAB BENCH**

Did you spot these scientific models in the colony modules on pages 28–31?

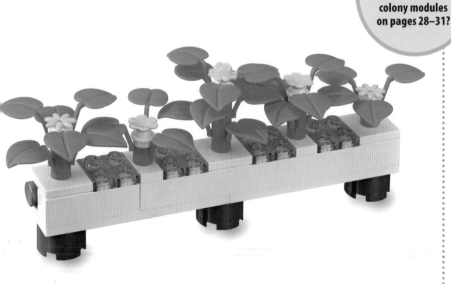

**PLANTING TABLE**

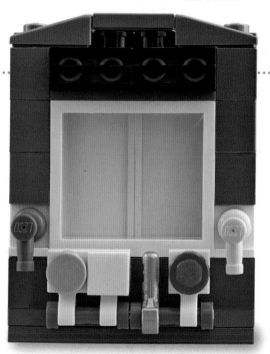

**FUME HOOD**

# An alien

An astronaut reports in with exciting news: alien life has been discovered on Volga! Build an alien life-form by combining pieces with interesting shapes and colors together with clip-and-bar connections for movement.

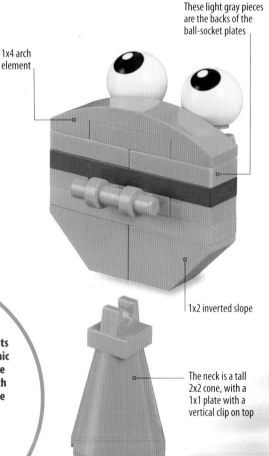

**START HERE**

The ring is made up of eight bar segments

## 1 Creature core

Attach two 2x2 round plates with holes underneath

Start with the core of your alien's body. Want it to have octopus-like legs? A plate with an octagonal ring provides a suitable circular shape with lots of attachment points.

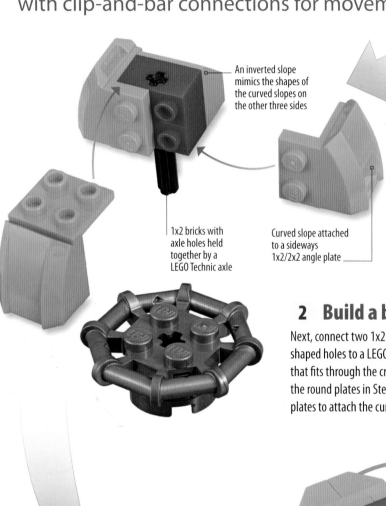

An inverted slope mimics the shapes of the curved slopes on the other three sides

1x2 bricks with axle holes held together by a LEGO Technic axle

Curved slope attached to a sideways 1x2/2x2 angle plate

## 2 Build a body

Next, connect two 1x2 bricks with cross-shaped holes to a LEGO Technic cross axle that fits through the cross-shaped holes on the round plates in Step 1. Use three angle plates to attach the curved body pieces.

These light gray pieces are the backs of the ball-socket plates

1x4 arch element

1x2 inverted slope

The neck is a tall 2x2 cone, with a 1x1 plate with a vertical clip on top

## 3 Add the head

Use plates, inverted slopes, and a small arch to build the head. A 1x2 handled bar plate creates a neck attachment, and two small 1x2 plates with ball sockets connect the eyes on top.

Printed LEGO® Mixels™ ball elements attach to LEGO Technic axle/ball pins. These snap into plates with ball-sockets to make the googly eyes.

## 4 Attach the legs

Each of the alien's legs is made from a 1x4 plate, 1x3 curved slope, a 1x1 slope, a 1x2 plate with a bar, a claw piece, and a robot arm. Remember, you'll need six of each part!

*JUST TWO MORE LEGS TO GO AND I'LL BE READY!*

Claw clips to bar on plate

Robot arm clips onto octagonal ring

You don't need to use these exact pieces for the leg-tips, you can make up your own

*GREETINGS, EARTHLING. I AM QUINLAG.*

*GREETINGS, QUINLAG. LET ME SHAKE YOU BY THE... ER... LEG?*

Curved slopes give the body an organic shape

It takes a lot of legs to hold up this alien's body!

## 5 Creature complete!

With its head and limbs attached, the alien creature is finished. Each leg has two clip-hinge joints and a rotation joint to let it stand and scuttle around. Time to introduce your new friend to the rest of your crew!

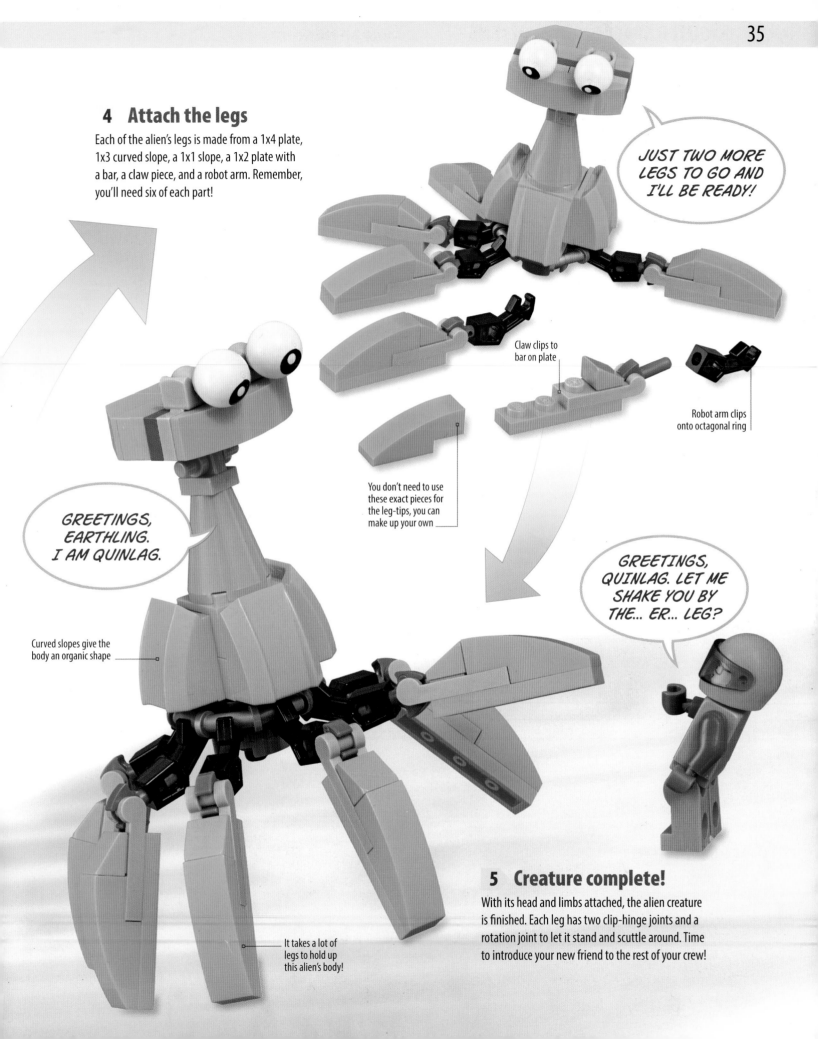

# Alien life

As the astronauts explore more of their new planet, they encounter more new aliens, each one stranger than the last. Populate your planet with plenty of fun and friendly extraterrestrial life-forms.

**WHAT'S NEXT?**

All of the aliens on this spread start with the same plate with octagonal ring as the one on page 34. Look for other pieces in your LEGO brick collection that will let you connect extra limbs.

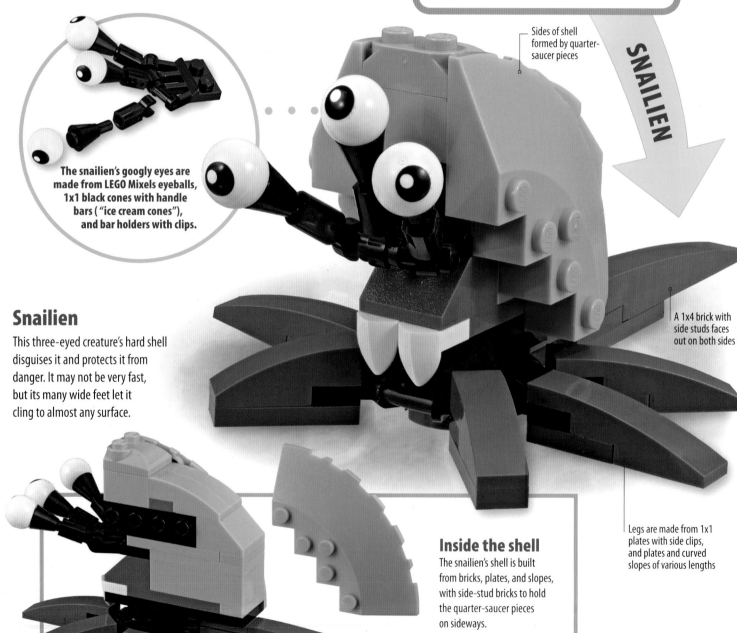

The snailien's googly eyes are made from LEGO Mixels eyeballs, 1x1 black cones with handle bars ( "ice cream cones"), and bar holders with clips.

Sides of shell formed by quarter-saucer pieces

SNAILIEN

A 1x4 brick with side studs faces out on both sides

## Snailien

This three-eyed creature's hard shell disguises it and protects it from danger. It may not be very fast, but its many wide feet let it cling to almost any surface.

**Inside the shell**
The snailien's shell is built from bricks, plates, and slopes, with side-stud bricks to hold the quarter-saucer pieces on sideways.

Legs are made from 1x1 plates with side clips, and plates and curved slopes of various lengths

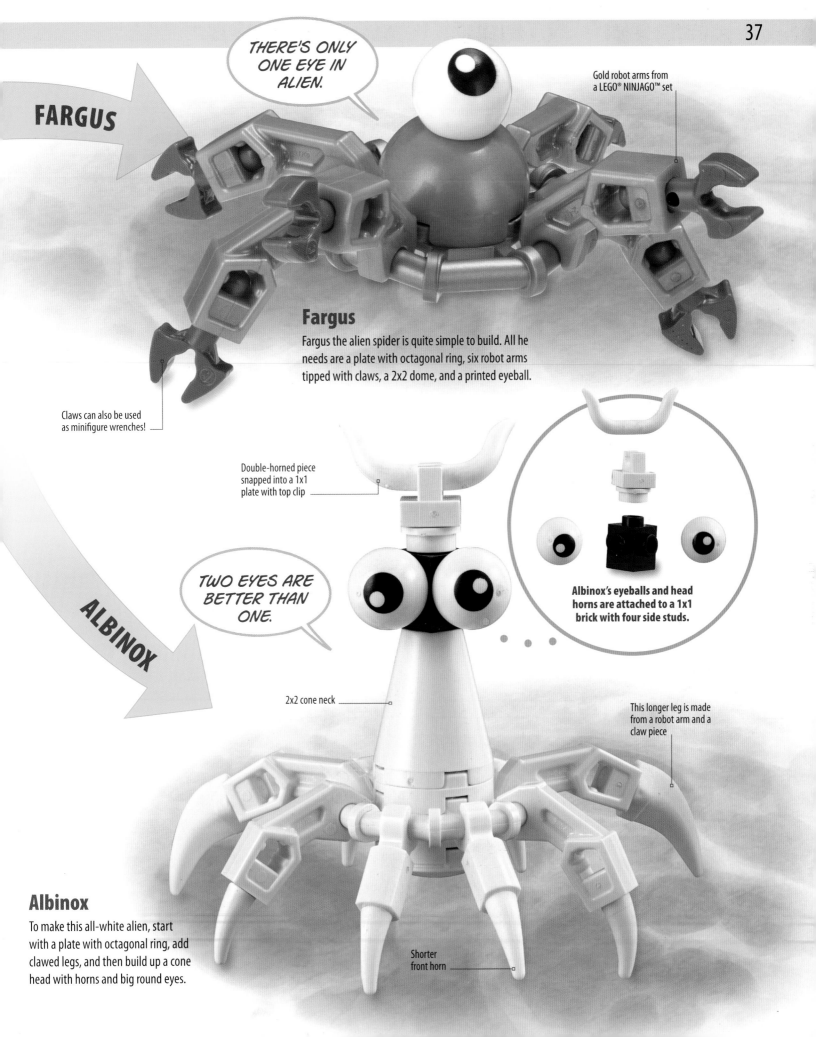

# FARGUS

THERE'S ONLY ONE EYE IN ALIEN.

Gold robot arms from a LEGO® NINJAGO™ set

## Fargus

Fargus the alien spider is quite simple to build. All he needs are a plate with octagonal ring, six robot arms tipped with claws, a 2x2 dome, and a printed eyeball.

Claws can also be used as minifigure wrenches!

Double-horned piece snapped into a 1x1 plate with top clip

TWO EYES ARE BETTER THAN ONE.

ALBINOX

**Albinox's eyeballs and head horns are attached to a 1x1 brick with four side studs.**

2x2 cone neck

This longer leg is made from a robot arm and a claw piece

## Albinox

To make this all-white alien, start with a plate with octagonal ring, add clawed legs, and then build up a cone head with horns and big round eyes.

Shorter front horn

# More alien life

The astronauts discover that the planet Volga is teeming with alien life, all scuttling, sliding, and flying around their world. What other otherworldy creatures can you dream up?

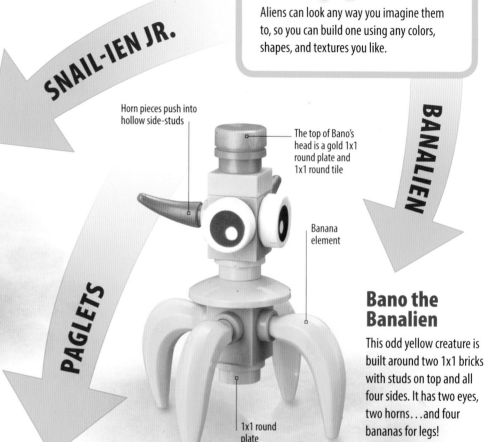

## WHAT'S NEXT?

Aliens can look any way you imagine them to, so you can build one using any colors, shapes, and textures you like.

### SNAIL-IEN JR.

### BANALIEN

### PAGLETS

## Snail-ien Jr.

This juvenile version of the Snailien from page 36 has a bigger shell, but only one eye! Soon it will lose its egg-teeth and start to grow into an adult.

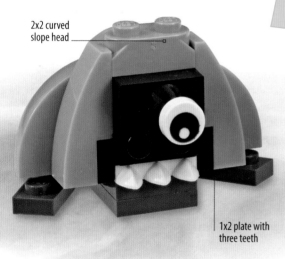

2x2 curved slope head

1x2 plate with three teeth

Horn pieces push into hollow side-studs

The top of Bano's head is a gold 1x1 round plate and 1x1 round tile

Banana element

1x1 round plate

## Bano the Banalien

This odd yellow creature is built around two 1x1 bricks with studs on top and all four sides. It has two eyes, two horns...and four bananas for legs!

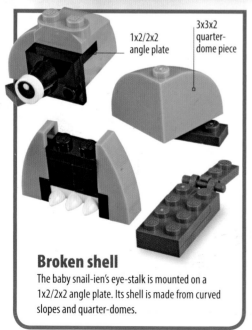

1x2/2x2 angle plate

3x3x2 quarter-dome piece

### Broken shell

The baby snail-ien's eye-stalk is mounted on a 1x2/2x2 angle plate. Its shell is made from curved slopes and quarter-domes.

## Paglets

Use the same pieces in different colors to create a swarm of matching alien creatures. The pointy-headed Paglets are curious about everything—and tend to scurry off with any unattached tools and food!

Eye can be positioned to look around

Crab claws are clips that can hold any bar-shaped element

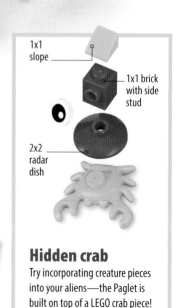

1x1 slope

1x1 brick with side stud

2x2 radar dish

### Hidden crab

Try incorporating creature pieces into your aliens—the Paglet is built on top of a LEGO crab piece!

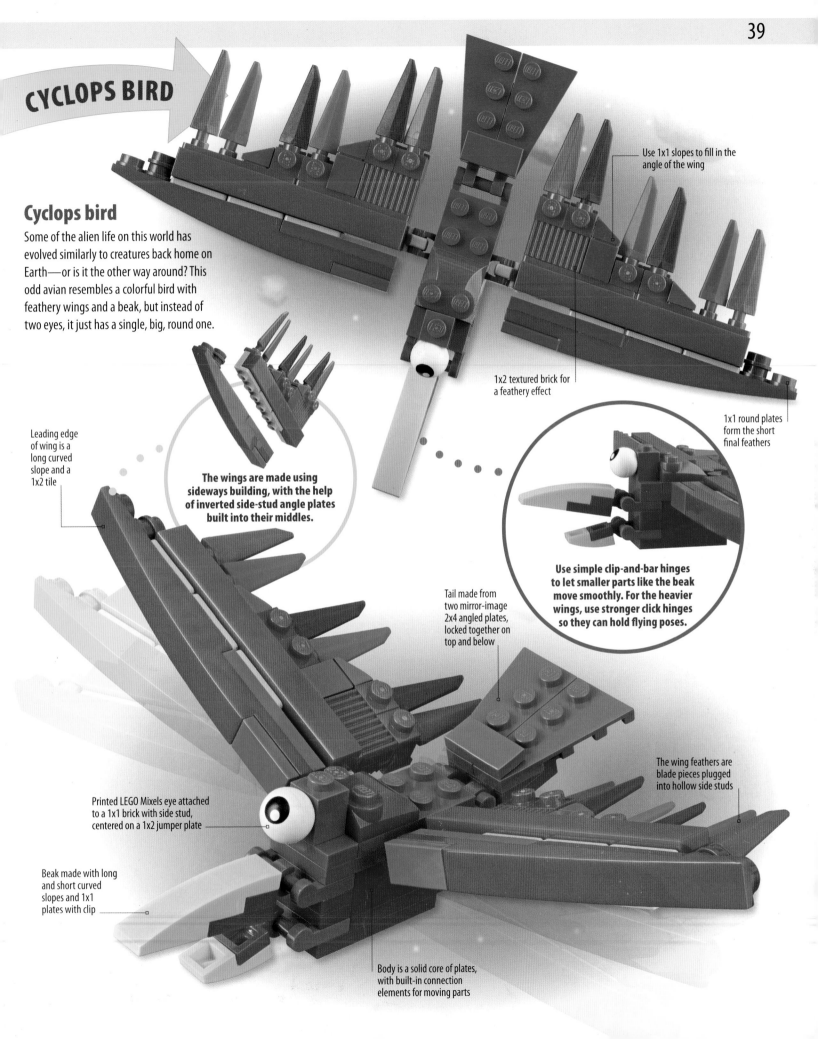

# CYCLOPS BIRD

## Cyclops bird

Some of the alien life on this world has evolved similarly to creatures back home on Earth—or is it the other way around? This odd avian resembles a colorful bird with feathery wings and a beak, but instead of two eyes, it just has a single, big, round one.

Use 1x1 slopes to fill in the angle of the wing

1x2 textured brick for a feathery effect

1x1 round plates form the short final feathers

Leading edge of wing is a long curved slope and a 1x2 tile

**The wings are made using sideways building, with the help of inverted side-stud angle plates built into their middles.**

**Use simple clip-and-bar hinges to let smaller parts like the beak move smoothly. For the heavier wings, use stronger click hinges so they can hold flying poses.**

Tail made from two mirror-image 2x4 angled plates, locked together on top and below

The wing feathers are blade pieces plugged into hollow side studs

Printed LEGO Mixels eye attached to a 1x1 brick with side stud, centered on a 1x2 jumper plate

Beak made with long and short curved slopes and 1x1 plates with clip

Body is a solid core of plates, with built-in connection elements for moving parts

# Space-plants and scenery

While some of the crew meet their new neighbors, others scout and catalog all of the new plants that they can find. Use your most unusual pieces to create weird and wonderful alien plants.

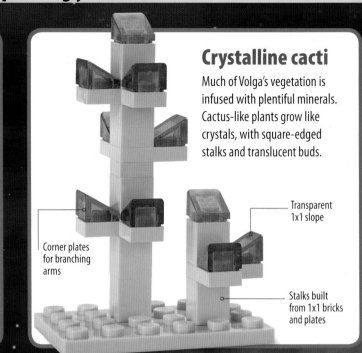

## Crystalline cacti

Much of Volga's vegetation is infused with plentiful minerals. Cactus-like plants grow like crystals, with square-edged stalks and translucent buds.

Corner plates for branching arms

Transparent 1x1 slope

Stalks built from 1x1 bricks and plates

Grass stem piece attaches to the stud in the center of the prickly bush

## Brush nest

Easily mistaken for seed pods, the spheres in the center of these brightly colored brushes are actually the eggs of an alien creature, protected by the plants' ensnaring vines.

Eggs are LEGO Technic balls

**These pieces have a click-hinge connector at each end.**

## Perilous plant

Not all plants are peaceful! A plate with octagonal ring and a set of cylinder click hinges let you create a hungry horticultural specimen that wouldn't mind trying just a taste of astronaut.

Make a hinge with a 1x2 plate with clips and a 1x2 plate with handled bar

A short, red cross axle connects the stem to a 1x2 brick with axle hole

Leaves made with 1x2 bricks with clips and 1x2 slopes

1x2 plate with three teeth

Large radar dish base

*AAARGH! THIS ONE HAS TEETH!*

## Cup plants

These plants use their cup-shaped tops to collect moisture from the air and store it inside their hollow stalks. Some of the planet's animals have learned to drink from their faucet-like branches.

Upside-down faucet piece

Stems attach to bricks with side studs

Base built as a wall of bricks on its side

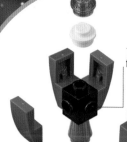

1x1 brick with four side studs

**This flower's petals are curved slopes attached to bricks with studs on top and all four sides.**

## Horn flowers

Volga's giant horn flowers resemble deep-sea plants from Earth. They can be found in all different sizes and keep growing throughout their lives, which can last for a century or longer.

Stamen made from a transparent cone and horn piece

Tall stem made from stacked cone pieces

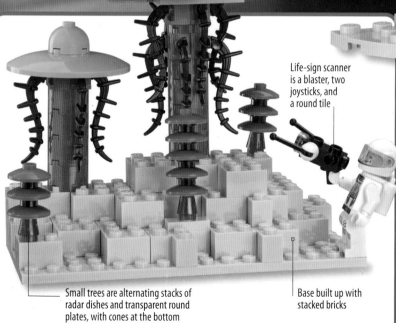

Life-sign scanner is a blaster, two joysticks, and a round tile

Small trees are alternating stacks of radar dishes and transparent round plates, with cones at the bottom

Base built up with stacked bricks

## Extra-terrestrial trees

These aren't flying saucers, but mushroom-like trees. The bigger trees' trunks are stacks of 2x2 round bricks with a LEGO Technic cross axle through the middle for stability. Tentacles attached to bricks with hollow side studs add to the alien look.

## Interplanetary landscapes

Build background scenery for your alien-planet scenes by using your bricks to make multiple levels, and then shaping the peaks with slope bricks of different angles and sizes.

A tall slope for a steep peak

A long slope for a gradual rise

# A micro-scale spaceship

The next assignment for the colony crew is to build a spacecraft for travel around their new planet. If you don't have a lot of bricks to build a big spaceship, make a little one in micro-scale instead.

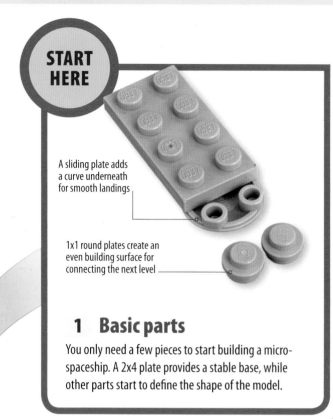

**START HERE**

A sliding plate adds a curve underneath for smooth landings

1x1 round plates create an even building surface for connecting the next level

## 1   Basic parts

You only need a few pieces to start building a micro-spaceship. A 2x4 plate provides a stable base, while other parts start to define the shape of the model.

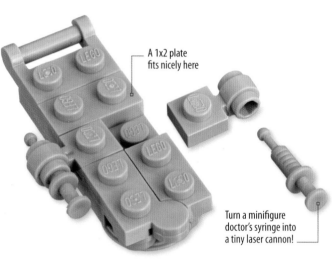

A 1x2 plate fits nicely here

Turn a minifigure doctor's syringe into a tiny laser cannon!

## 2   Space shape

A folded hinge plate gives your micro-ship a pointed nose, and a 1x2 plate with bar creates a clip connection point at the back. Adding 1x1 plates with side rings let you attach cool space-age details.

*Small, detailed LEGO elements become big, detailed parts on a micro-model. What pieces in your collection could be part of a miniature vehicle?*

*I'LL HANDLE THIS.*

Plates with handled bars create mounts for wings

A 1x2 plate with side bars gives a large spaceship tiny lasers...or a little spaceship gigantic ones!

## 3   Color and details

The next set of pieces continues to add to your micro-spaceship's details, while also giving it an eye-catching color scheme. Especially useful are bars to let you attach the wings.

## 4 Taking wing

Build a pair of mirror-image wings and clip them into place on the model's sides. Attach some rocket engines to the handled bar at the back, too!

1x2 click-hinge plate adds a decorative detail

This bracket is usually used for attaching backpacks to minifigures!

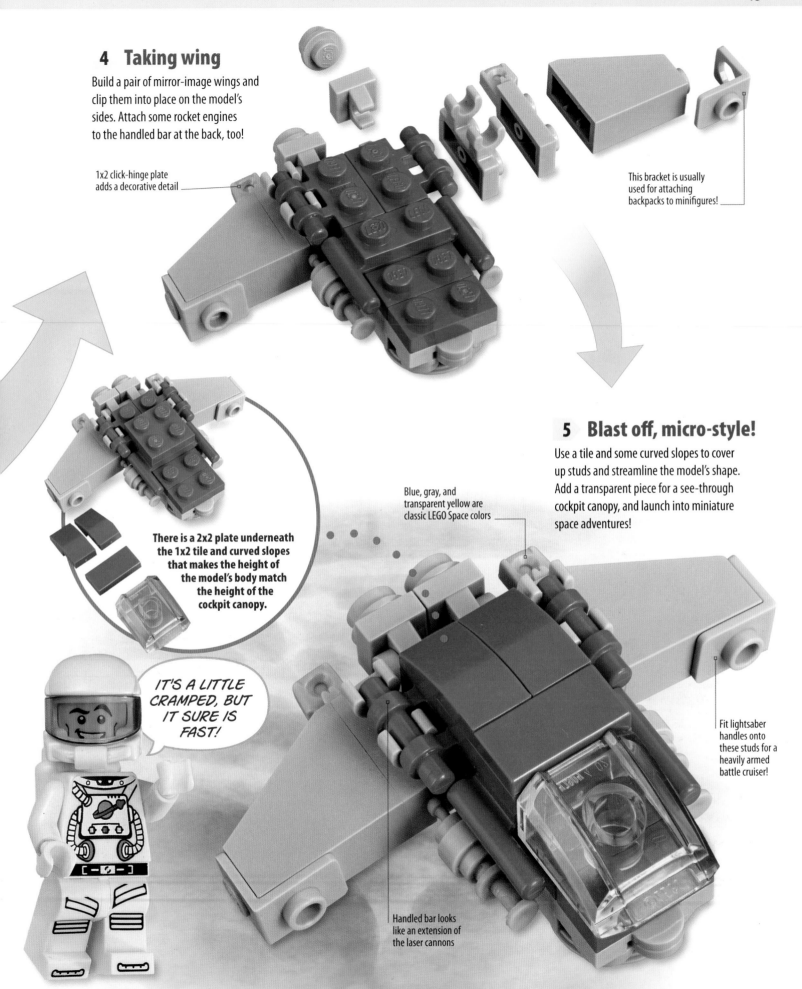

There is a 2x2 plate underneath the 1x2 tile and curved slopes that makes the height of the model's body match the height of the cockpit canopy.

## 5 Blast off, micro-style!

Use a tile and some curved slopes to cover up studs and streamline the model's shape. Add a transparent piece for a see-through cockpit canopy, and launch into miniature space adventures!

Blue, gray, and transparent yellow are classic LEGO Space colors

IT'S A LITTLE CRAMPED, BUT IT SURE IS FAST!

Fit lightsaber handles onto these studs for a heavily armed battle cruiser!

Handled bar looks like an extension of the laser cannons

# Micro-space fleet

Why stop at one micro-spaceship when you can assemble an entire fleet? You can build a whole armada of fighters, transport vessels, starships, and shuttles.

**WHAT'S NEXT?**

Like the spaceship on the last page, these micro-ships use small pieces in interesting and inventive new ways.

ZYCON SHUTTLE

ONYX GUNSHIP

Flag pieces for tail fins

Wing cannons are minifigure screwdrivers plugged into 1x1 plates with side rings

## *Zycon* shuttle

You can build miniature versions of bigger models. This micro-scale version of the expedition team's shuttle (you'll see it in full-size on pages 48–49) captures all of the important shapes and details of the bigger model.

Pointed tooth plates give the pods their shape

Flags clipped to 1x1 handled bar plates for wings

1x2 brick with side studs and stand

A tooth plate sits on top

A transparent yellow 1x1 plate stacked on a black one extends the length of the cockpit

## Controlled explosion

Like many micro-models, the secret to this spaceship's construction is the piece with side studs at its core, as this exploded view shows.

Transparent 1x1 slope cockpit

## *Onyx* gunship

Try making a micro-model that's as small as possible, but still recognizable as a spaceship. Little angled pieces will really come in handy here!

# THE CAYMAN

## The *Cayman*

Not every micro-scale model needs to be tiny! Even shrunk down, the crew's interstellar starship is still a sizeable model, with room for lots of detail elements.

2x2 radar dishes and a 1x1 round plate add surface detailing

Pieces with sideways studs let you build out the hull sideways

*CAYMAN TO MARAUDER...BIT OF A SPACE JAM.*

**REAR VIEW**

MARAUDER

## Marauder

With the right parts, you can make really unique and exciting micro-scale spacecraft designs, like this powerful-looking ship with its forward wings and double-cockpits.

Cockpit section built around 1x1 bricks with studs on all four sides

Joystick is a giant antenna

*LET'S TAKE THE MILKY HIGH WAY.*

Use 1x1 slopes for an angled hull

**REAR VIEW**

# Micro-scale space buildings

Now you can use your bricks to create an interactive miniature universe for your micro-spaceships. Just use the same micro-scale techniques to build towers, launch pads, and other outer-space locations.

The tower's five sides are connected by clip hinges.

A tall antenna is clipped to one of the roof points via a robot arm piece

Angled plates clipped to the top bend inward to form a cone

### Space city tower

This micro-model takes the idea of a modern city apartment building and gives it a sci-fi twist. Its five sides snap together to make a pentagon-shaped, hi-tech high-rise.

*IT'S GOT A GREAT VIEW OF THE LEGO NEBULA.*

Transparent 1x2 tiles for panoramic apartment windows

Sloped pieces make a wide support base

**FLAT VIEW**

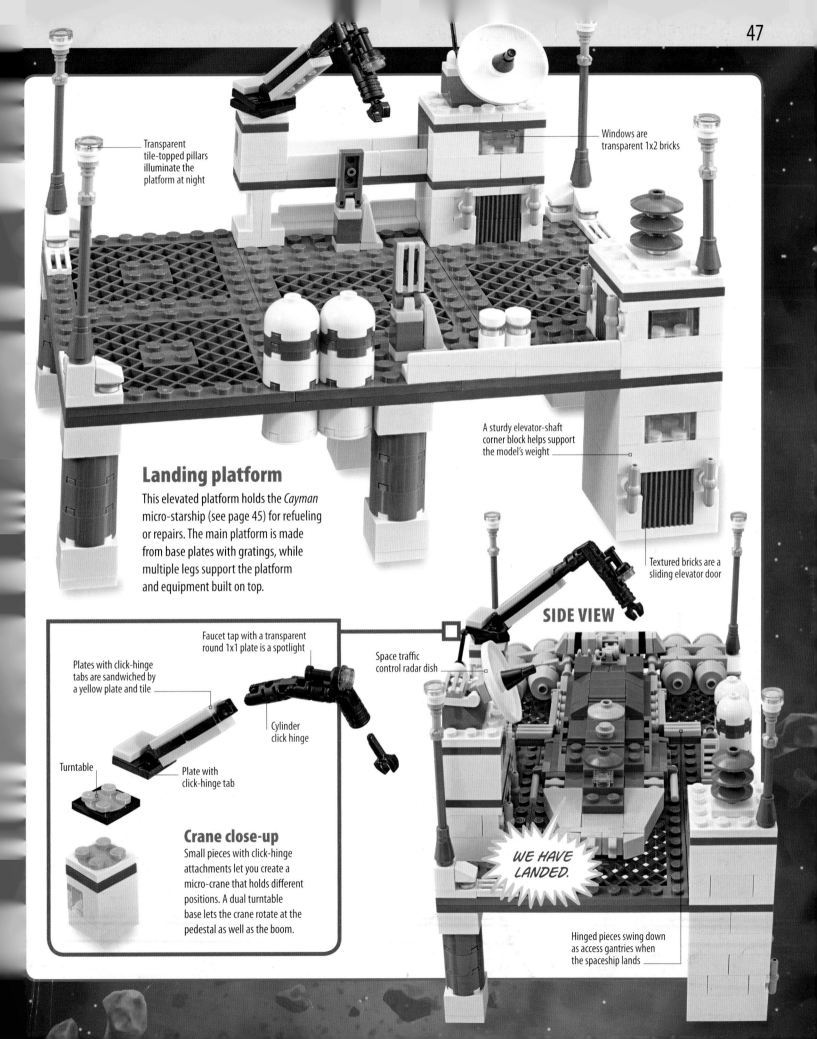

Transparent tile-topped pillars illuminate the platform at night

Windows are transparent 1x2 bricks

A sturdy elevator-shaft corner block helps support the model's weight

Textured bricks are a sliding elevator door

## Landing platform

This elevated platform holds the *Cayman* micro-starship (see page 45) for refueling or repairs. The main platform is made from base plates with gratings, while multiple legs support the platform and equipment built on top.

Faucet tap with a transparent round 1x1 plate is a spotlight

Plates with click-hinge tabs are sandwiched by a yellow plate and tile

Space traffic control radar dish

**SIDE VIEW**

Cylinder click hinge

Turntable

Plate with click-hinge tab

## Crane close-up

Small pieces with click-hinge attachments let you create a micro-crane that holds different positions. A dual turntable base lets the crane rotate at the pedestal as well as the boom.

WE HAVE LANDED.

Hinged pieces swing down as access gantries when the spaceship lands

# Zycon shuttle

After weeks of work the new space colony on Volga is nearly complete. The *Zycon* cargo starship just needs to return to Earth to pick up some final supplies.

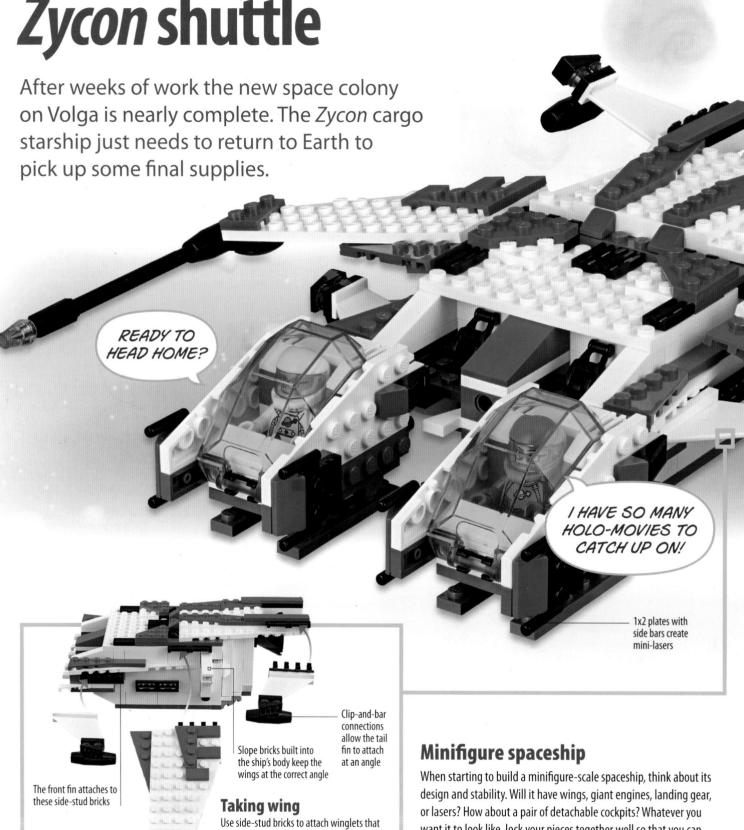

READY TO HEAD HOME?

I HAVE SO MANY HOLO-MOVIES TO CATCH UP ON!

1x2 plates with side bars create mini-lasers

The front fin attaches to these side-stud bricks

Slope bricks built into the ship's body keep the wings at the correct angle

Clip-and-bar connections allow the tail fin to attach at an angle

### Taking wing
Use side-stud bricks to attach winglets that stick straight out, and clip-and-bar hinges for angled wings and tail fins.

## Minifigure spaceship
When starting to build a minifigure-scale spaceship, think about its design and stability. Will it have wings, giant engines, landing gear, or lasers? How about a pair of detachable cockpits? Whatever you want it to look like, lock your pieces together well so that you can pick it up and have fun "swooshing" it around!

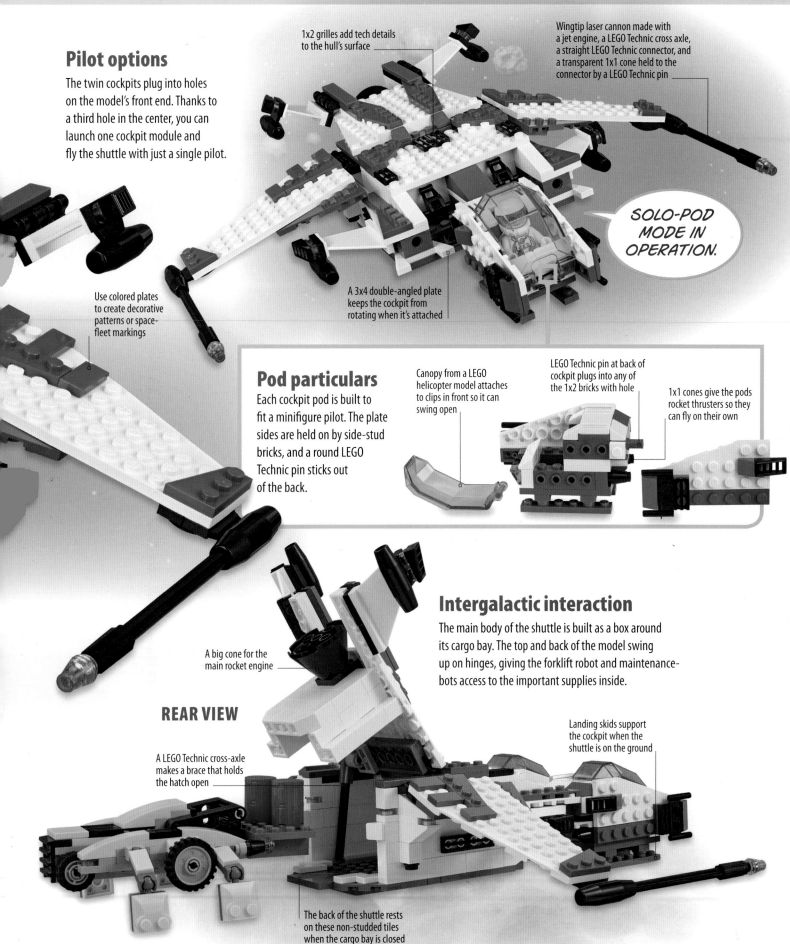

## Pilot options

The twin cockpits plug into holes on the model's front end. Thanks to a third hole in the center, you can launch one cockpit module and fly the shuttle with just a single pilot.

1x2 grilles add tech details to the hull's surface

Wingtip laser cannon made with a jet engine, a LEGO Technic cross axle, a straight LEGO Technic connector, and a transparent 1x1 cone held to the connector by a LEGO Technic pin

*SOLO-POD MODE IN OPERATION.*

Use colored plates to create decorative patterns or space-fleet markings

A 3x4 double-angled plate keeps the cockpit from rotating when it's attached

## Pod particulars

Each cockpit pod is built to fit a minifigure pilot. The plate sides are held on by side-stud bricks, and a round LEGO Technic pin sticks out of the back.

Canopy from a LEGO helicopter model attaches to clips in front so it can swing open

LEGO Technic pin at back of cockpit plugs into any of the 1x2 bricks with hole

1x1 cones give the pods rocket thrusters so they can fly on their own

## Intergalactic interaction

The main body of the shuttle is built as a box around its cargo bay. The top and back of the model swing up on hinges, giving the forklift robot and maintenance-bots access to the important supplies inside.

A big cone for the main rocket engine

**REAR VIEW**

Landing skids support the cockpit when the shuttle is on the ground

A LEGO Technic cross-axle makes a brace that holds the hatch open

The back of the shuttle rests on these non-studded tiles when the cargo bay is closed

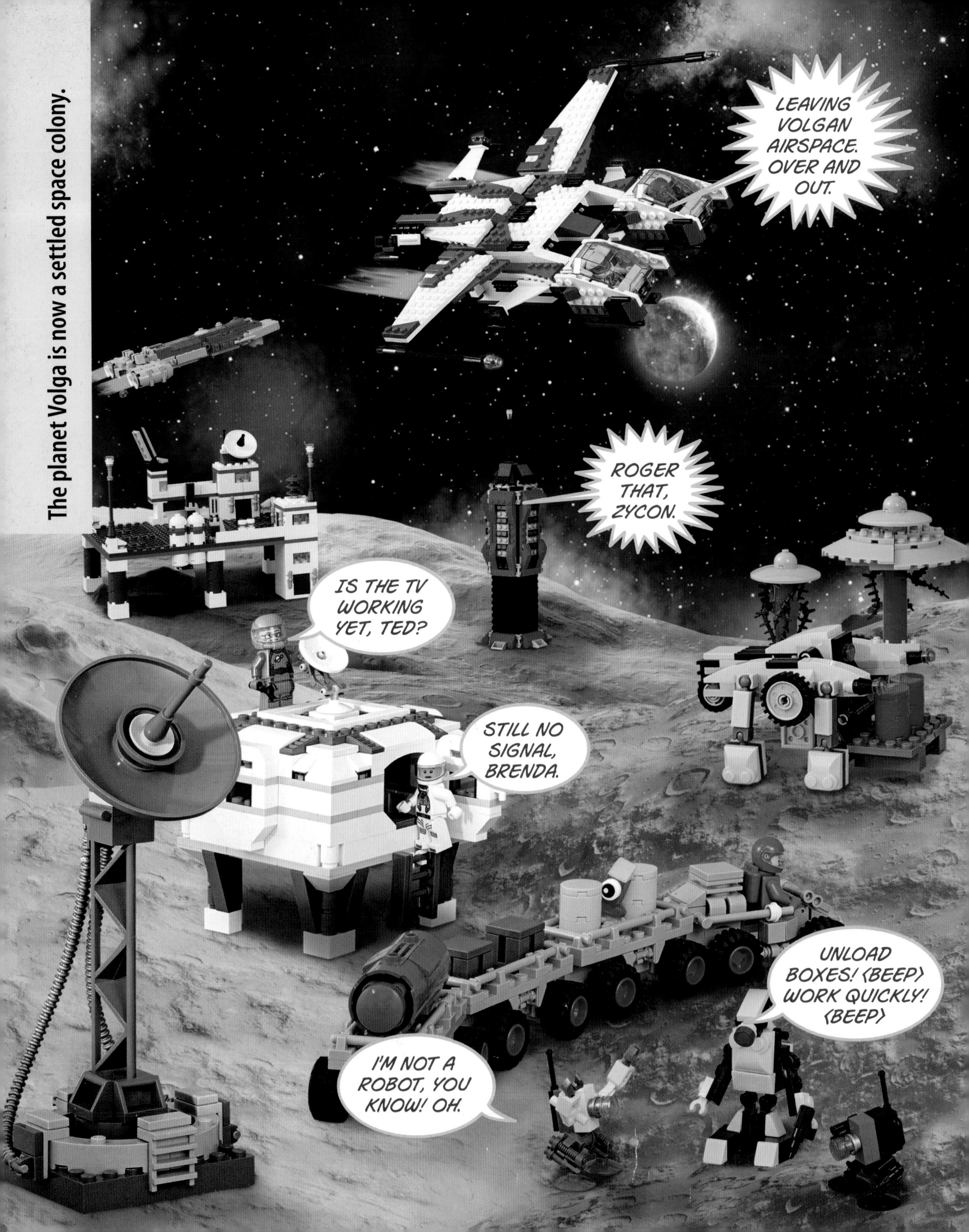


The planet Volga is now a settled space colony.

# MODERN METROPOLIS

Do you know what a city planner sees when she looks at a big, jumbled pile of bricks? A gleaming modern city, with homes, stores, offices, and everything in between. To make a metropolis, you need architects, planners, and workers. And what you need most of all is a creative mind that can dream up awesome buildings, and then build them into reality. Are you up to the challenge? Let's get started!

# A basic building

The city planner begins the construction of her new city with a single modular building. By following the same basic steps but changing the colors and details around, you can connect a few similar buildings together to make an entire city block.

**START HERE**

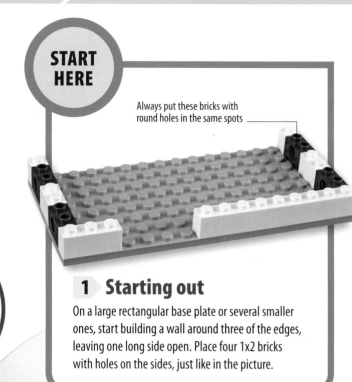

Always put these bricks with round holes in the same spots

### 1 Starting out

On a large rectangular base plate or several smaller ones, start building a wall around three of the edges, leaving one long side open. Place four 1x2 bricks with holes on the sides, just like in the picture.

**If you don't have these special 1x4 plates with two studs, you could use a smooth 1x2 tile with a studded 1x1 plate at each end instead.**

### 2 Build up the walls

Build the three walls up to a height of six bricks, laying a long brick across the open side at the top. Add a layer of smooth tiles, with just four studs sticking up.

Use a LEGO door, or you could leave an open space

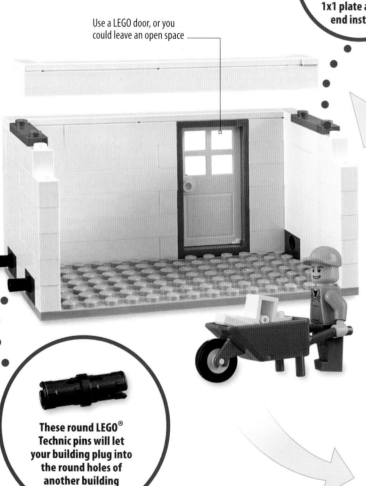

This window is two bricks up from the base plate and fits in a space that is four studs across and three bricks high

**These round LEGO® Technic pins will let your building plug into the round holes of another building next to it.**

### 3 A second module

Now build a second building module, just like the first one...but instead of a door, build a window into the long wall at the front of the building.

Keep adding more stories, or put a plate on top as a roof

ERM, I THINK WE FORGOT SOMETHING... STAIRS!

## 4 Building complete

With two modules, you've put together a great two-story building. Would you rather make it three stories tall, or even four? Just build more modules and stack them on top. You can make longer buildings, too, by joining the modules side-by-side.

The sturdiest walls have staggered rows of bricks just like real houses

A 1x1 round plate makes a good doorknob

OOPS.

## SIDE-BY-SIDE

Leave a door-shaped hole in these connecting walls to let your minifigures walk between the rooms

The modules connect side by side by snapping the LEGO Technic pins into the round holes at the base of the walls

With one door, these modules look like one long house. Add a door to the second module, and they're next-door neighbors!

# Modular buildings

These buildings were all constructed in a modular style similar to the ones on the previous page. Stacking modules on top of each other creates office blocks and other tall buildings found all around town.

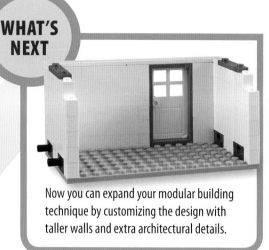

**WHAT'S NEXT**

Now you can expand your modular building technique by customizing the design with taller walls and extra architectural details.

OFFICE BLOCK

*IT'S LONELY AT THE TOP.*

With modular building, you can add more floors as the company grows

1x6x5 panels let you build large sections of wall quickly. Use clear ones for big windows!

The wall of the reception floor is stepped in to create an entrance with flower boxes

The company president gets the whole upper floor to himself

*LANCE ALWAYS FORGETS MY SUGAR.*

**REAR VIEW**

## Office block

This modern office building looks organized and professional. Its modules appear similar from the outside, but on the inside each has its own particular function to keep the business running smoothly.

**Look at pages 64–67 to see some of the furniture on these pages in more detail.**

## Library

This library is three modules high, with an extra rooftop section on top. Like the real thing, it has a checkout desk, a research room, and lots of books to borrow and read.

LIBRARY

Use slopes of differing heights and colors to make an angled rooftop

Alternate rows of regular and textured bricks, such as log bricks, create interestingly patterned walls

Keep track of the time with a printed 2x2 round clock tile attached to bricks with sideways-pointing studs

LEGO books don't attach to studs, so build shelves or storage racks to hold them

YEP, OLD NEWS IS THE BEST NEWS.

The windows stick out from the wall with the aid of 2x2 slopes above and 2x2 inverted slopes below

Book scanner is made from a sci-fi ray gun with a transparent red 1x1 tile on the end

**REAR VIEW**

# City buildings

As the city planner's metropolis grows, more building shapes start to pop up. They might all be built around basic box shapes, but the colors, details, and piece selection make each of these city buildings unique.

**CORNER SHOP**

**WHAT'S NEXT?**

Combining boxes in different ways means you can build in a variety of shapes, including making some more complex buildings.

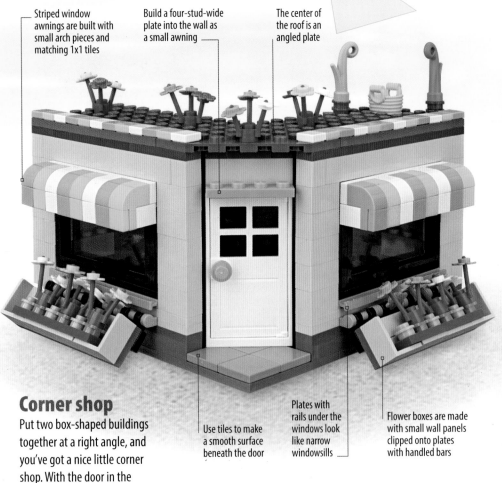

Striped window awnings are built with small arch pieces and matching 1x1 tiles

Build a four-stud-wide plate into the wall as a small awning

The center of the roof is an angled plate

By making the walls two studs thick, you can set the windows back from the outside edge and strengthen the building's structure

## Corner shop
Put two box-shaped buildings together at a right angle, and you've got a nice little corner shop. With the door in the middle and both sides matching, it looks like it's all one store.

Use tiles to make a smooth surface beneath the door

Plates with rails under the windows look like narrow windowsills

Flower boxes are made with small wall panels clipped onto plates with handled bars

Build a sidewalk in front with large tiles

## Hospital

Combine multiple boxes into one building with an unusual shape. A modern hospital has many different sections, and each can be represented by a box of a different shape and style.

HOSPITAL

A window at the back adds more light inside

**REAR VIEW**

The smaller top floor is set one stud back from the ground floor

*BONES? I ALWAYS THOUGHT I WAS HOLLOW INSIDE!*

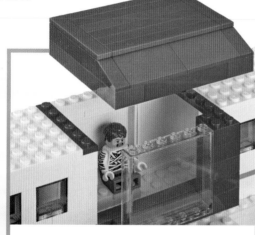

### Feature window

The red section is the eye-catching center of the building. Slopes and inverted slopes help to make an extra-big box that sticks out beyond the edges of the upper level.

Tall, thin windows make a building look important and longer than it really is

Patients might drive up, walk in, or arrive by ambulance, so include several entrances

# City museum

This ornate city museum is an example of how you can make a simple box-shaped building more exciting by adding interesting architecture. Check your collection for pieces with special shapes and textures.

Use clear slopes for skylight windows set into the museum roof.

Carvings are 1x1 round plates, bricks, and cones

Plates with rails for extra details

Square columns are stacks of 1x2 textured bricks

Use tooth plates for column decorations

*I JUST LOVE LOOKING AT OLD BRICKS.*

Add a round tile for the door handles

Slopes and shiny tiles create white marble steps

## Classical architecture

Many of the details on this grand building are inspired by Classical Greek and Roman architecture. These include the columns at the front, the fancy portico over the doorway built from round bricks and cones, and the "frieze" around the sides made of bumpy log bricks.

An arch above the window for classic elegance

This ornate dragon window is found in LEGO® NINJAGO™ sets

Portico columns made from 2x2 textured round bricks

**NIGHT VIEW**

## Gallery of the past

Your museum will be even more believable if artifacts can be glimpsed through its windows. Create some mini-galleries inside!

Attach historical minifigure accessories to the wall with side-stud bricks

Use 1x2 transparent bricks to make display cases

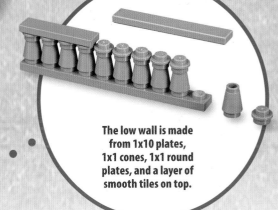

**The low wall is made from 1x10 plates, 1x1 cones, 1x1 round plates, and a layer of smooth tiles on top.**

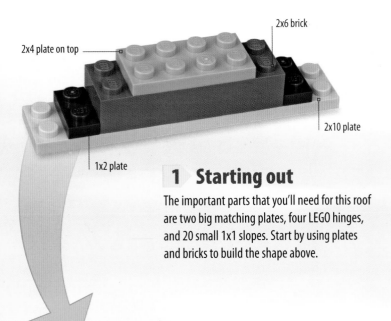

2x4 plate on top

2x6 brick

2x10 plate

1x2 plate

# Building roofs

One of the city planner's favorite parts of a building is its roof. A roof can be simple or fancy, angled or flat. Here are two easy rooftop designs that you can use to top off your own metropolis models!

## 1 Starting out

The important parts that you'll need for this roof are two big matching plates, four LEGO hinges, and 20 small 1x1 slopes. Start by using plates and bricks to build the shape above.

## 2 Building up

Next, place the 1x1 slopes as shown. When properly arranged, they will form a bed to support the shape of the angled rooftop. If you don't have this many slopes in the same color, mix them up!

Put the hinges on the sides first, and then connect the roof plates

## 3 Final stage

Add the two-piece hinges so that they point in opposite directions. Attach the rooftop plates across two of these builds, and you're done!

Make sure you snap the hinges together the right way around

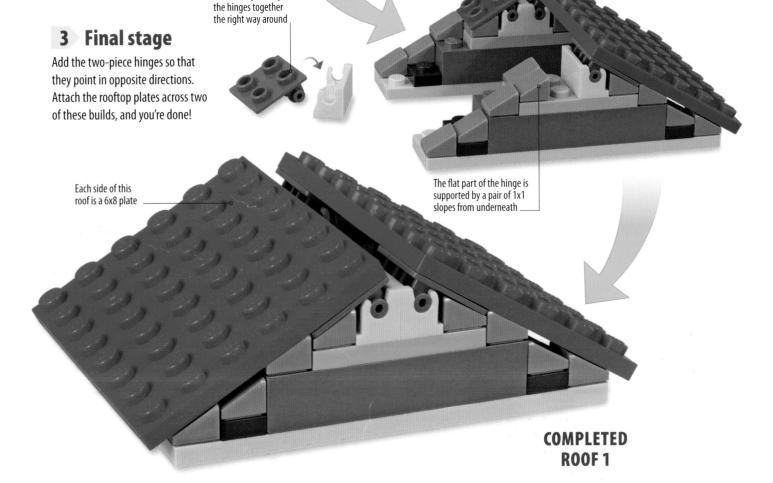

Each side of this roof is a 6x8 plate

The flat part of the hinge is supported by a pair of 1x1 slopes from underneath

**COMPLETED ROOF 1**

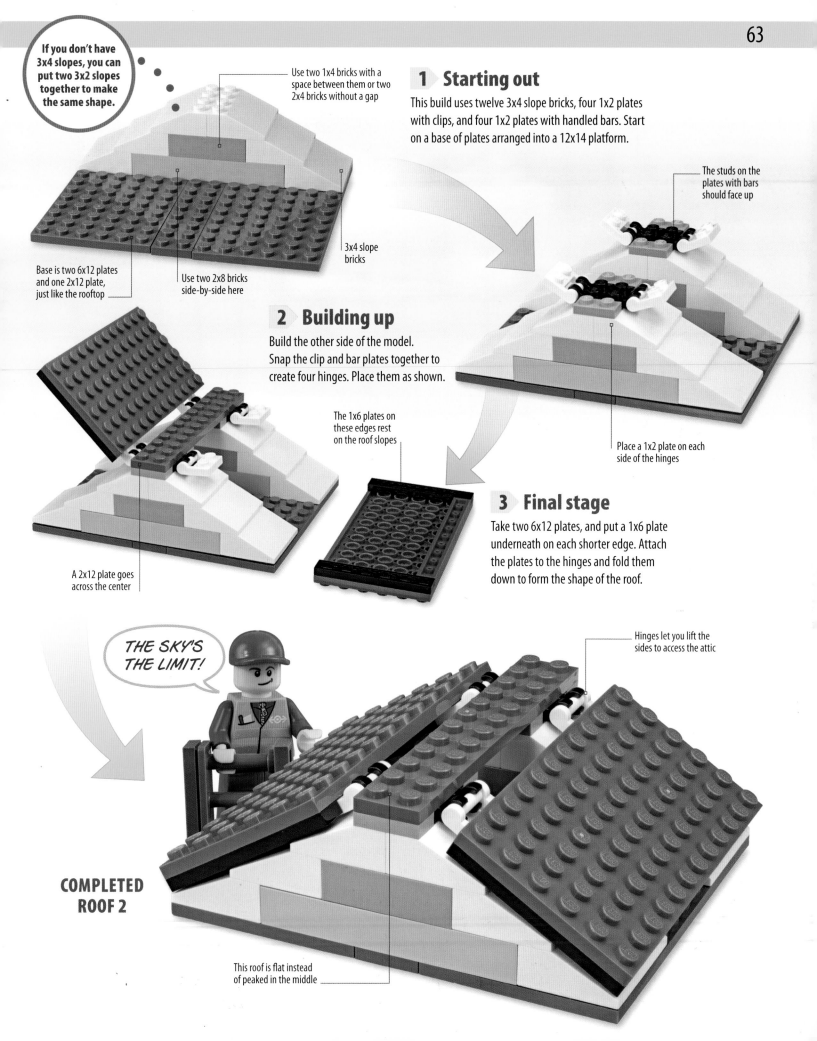

If you don't have 3x4 slopes, you can put two 3x2 slopes together to make the same shape.

Use two 1x4 bricks with a space between them or two 2x4 bricks without a gap

## 1 Starting out

This build uses twelve 3x4 slope bricks, four 1x2 plates with clips, and four 1x2 plates with handled bars. Start on a base of plates arranged into a 12x14 platform.

The studs on the plates with bars should face up

3x4 slope bricks

Base is two 6x12 plates and one 2x12 plate, just like the rooftop

Use two 2x8 bricks side-by-side here

## 2 Building up

Build the other side of the model. Snap the clip and bar plates together to create four hinges. Place them as shown.

The 1x6 plates on these edges rest on the roof slopes

Place a 1x2 plate on each side of the hinges

## 3 Final stage

Take two 6x12 plates, and put a 1x6 plate underneath on each shorter edge. Attach the plates to the hinges and fold them down to form the shape of the roof.

A 2x12 plate goes across the center

Hinges let you lift the sides to access the attic

THE SKY'S THE LIMIT!

**COMPLETED ROOF 2**

This roof is flat instead of peaked in the middle

# Tables and chairs gallery

Without chairs, we would have to stand up all the time... and think of how messy mealtimes would be without tables! Build some furniture to make your citizens' lives more comfortable.

1x2 plate armrest

Pin fits into this 1x2 brick with hole

1x4 arch

**The rocker and armrest on this rocking chair are built upside down and attach to the seat using a LEGO Technic pin.**

**THIS CHAIR ROCKS.**

**ROCKING CHAIR**

**DINING CHAIR**

**Spot this table and stools in the library on page 57.**

**STOOL**

**CAFÉ TABLE AND STOOLS**

**THANK GOODNESS FOR THIS QUIET CORNER.**

**FANCY CHAISE LONGUE**

**CORNER SOFA**

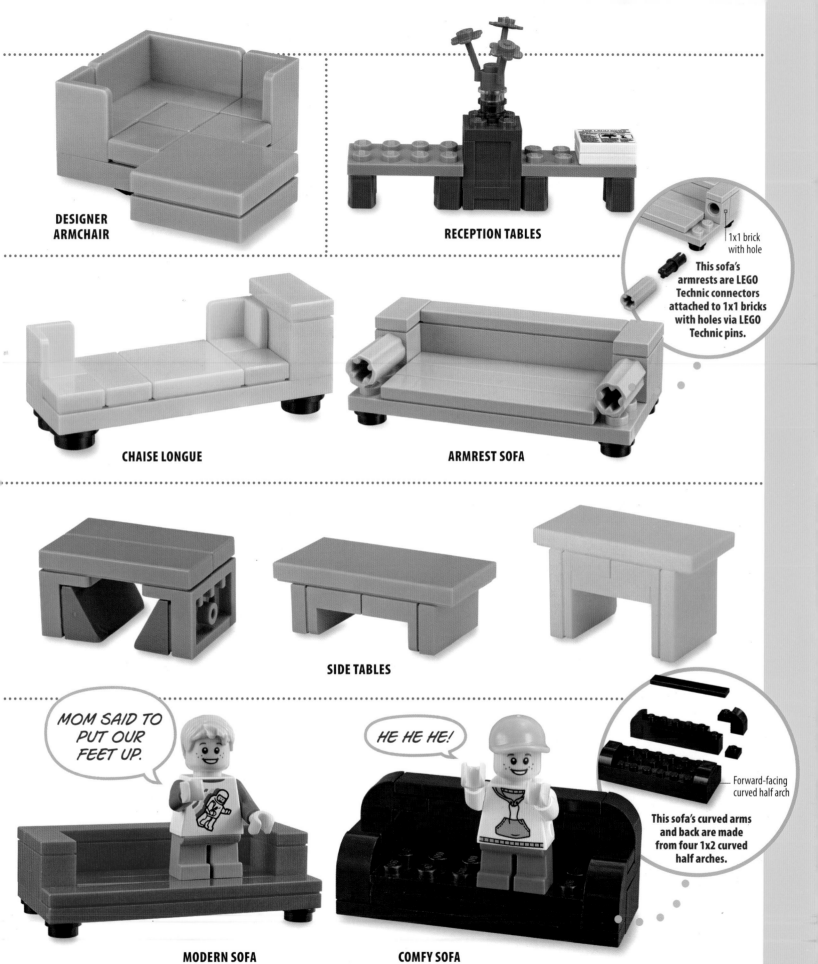

**DESIGNER ARMCHAIR**

**RECEPTION TABLES**

1x1 brick with hole

This sofa's armrests are LEGO Technic connectors attached to 1x1 bricks with holes via LEGO Technic pins.

**CHAISE LONGUE**

**ARMREST SOFA**

**SIDE TABLES**

MOM SAID TO PUT OUR FEET UP.

HE HE HE!

Forward-facing curved half arch

This sofa's curved arms and back are made from four 1x2 curved half arches.

**MODERN SOFA**

**COMFY SOFA**

# Furniture gallery

Here's a collection of common and not-so-common objects from inside city buildings. Use these small but detailed builds to make your building interiors more lifelike and fun.

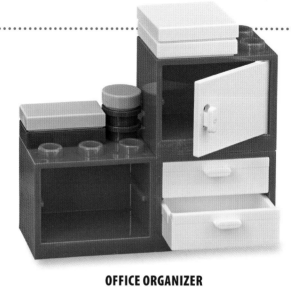

**OFFICE ORGANIZER**

**BEDSIDE TABLE**

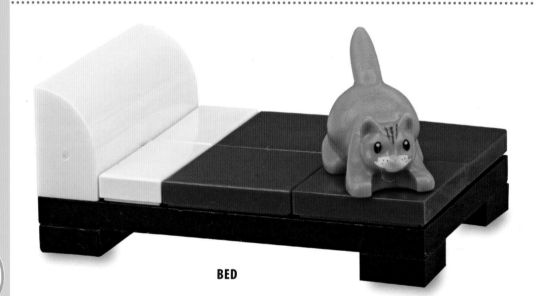

**BED**

*THIS ONE'S A GREAT READ!*

**BOOKSTAND**

**BOOKSHELF**

**SHELF UNIT**

**COLORED LIGHTS**

**DESK LAMP**

**SOLAR LIGHT**

**ADJUSTABLE LAMP**

See some of these models inside the buildings on pages 56 and 57.

I'LL SWAP YOU SOME FILES FOR A CROISSANT.

**OFFICE DESKS AND FURNITURE**

**WATER COOLERS**

**FLAT-SCREEN TV**

# Around the city

What other models can you build to go outside the buildings and on the streets of your city? Here are some familiar sights that you'll be likely to find in any good metropolis.

## ATM

Do your citizens need cash in a hurry? Place an automated teller machine against the side of a building, or build it directly into the wall.

**This sign is held on by an angle plate, but you can use any piece with side studs.**

Keypad is a 2x2 slope brick with a sticker attached

A 1x2 plate with rail keeps the money tile from going so far in that it gets stuck

## Bike racks

How do you store a LEGO bicycle so that it doesn't block the sidewalk? These racks solve the same problem in two different creative ways.

This rack uses 1x2 plates with hook-shaped bars to suspend the bikes end-to-end at an angle

**END-TO-END RACK**

This version uses L-shaped bar elements plugged into side-stud bricks to prop the bikes up side-by-side

**SIDE-BY-SIDE RACK**

**This headlight brick is filled out by a 1x1 plate.**

## Fire hydrants

All you need to build a fire hydrant are a 1x1 round brick, some 1x1 round plates, and a 1x1 brick with one or more side studs.

A 1x1 plate with clip holds the phone when it's not in use

**The kiosk's phone details attach to the sideways-facing studs of an angle plate bracket built into the back of the model.**

Kiosk "buttons" are a printed 1x2 tile

This phone booth has a door for privacy

*...BUT WHERE ARE THE APPS?*

*THIS IS HOW WE USED TO TALK ON THE PHONE, TIMMY.*

1x2x3 C-shaped windows in the middle make space for a minifigure's arms

## Public telephones

In the days before cell phones, this is how people used to stay in touch when they weren't at home! A public telephone will add a little color to your city street. Here are two different ways to build one.

Slopes at base support the wider top

**KIOSK**

**BOOTH**

## Puppet show

A puppet theater will keep your city's kids smiling. The puppets are minifigure heads fitted on the ends of flick-fire missile pieces!

Back of 1x1 side-stud bricks

*YIKES!*

*GRRRRR.*

**Horns pushed into hollow side-stud bricks hold up the minifigure-cape curtain.**

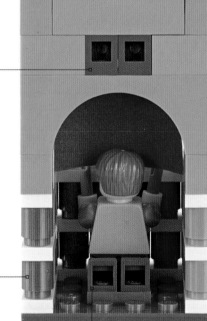

Base is a three-walled box made with plates and 1x1 round bricks

Turn minifigure legs around for a kneeling pose

**REAR VIEW**

THERE'S NO TIME TO WASTE!

START HERE

# Making a car

Now that the city planner has built her metropolis, she needs to create some cars and trucks so her citizens can get around easily. Start with a sport utility vehicle (SUV) that can handle the roads inside and outside the city.

Wheels attach to 2x4 plates with built-in LEGO Technic pins

## 1 Chassis

A strong car model needs a strong chassis underneath. Pick out two long plates and four sturdy wheels to attach to them. You're building an SUV, so make sure your tires are rugged.

## 2 Inner structure

Next, start putting together the underlying structure of the car. Protect the wheels with mudguards, and use sideways building to attach bumpers and lights at the front and back.

Leave space for a minifigure to sit behind the steering wheel

Looking for some help with bumpers? Check out pages 74 and 75.

This 1x6x1 inverted roof tile fits nicely between the wheels and around the mudguards on either side.

Use an angled plate for a tapering front end

This is a good time to test-fit your driver

## 3 Taking form

Begin to develop the car's shape and color scheme. Pieces with angled edges will help to keep it from looking too square and blocky. It's especially important to lock down the mudguards so they won't pop loose.

A sandwiched black plate creates a stripe on the side of the car

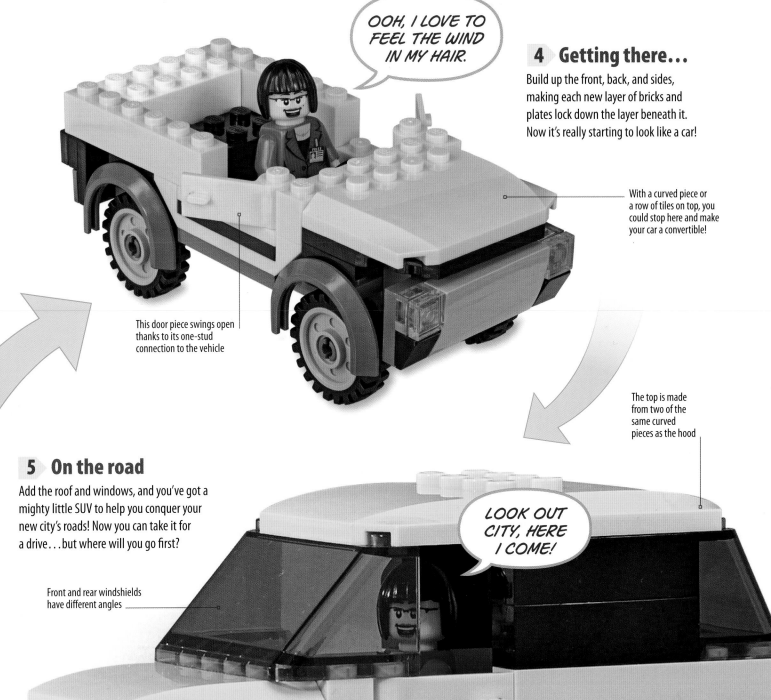

OOH, I LOVE TO FEEL THE WIND IN MY HAIR.

## 4 Getting there...

Build up the front, back, and sides, making each new layer of bricks and plates lock down the layer beneath it. Now it's really starting to look like a car!

With a curved piece or a row of tiles on top, you could stop here and make your car a convertible!

This door piece swings open thanks to its one-stud connection to the vehicle

The top is made from two of the same curved pieces as the hood

## 5 On the road

Add the roof and windows, and you've got a mighty little SUV to help you conquer your new city's roads! Now you can take it for a drive...but where will you go first?

LOOK OUT CITY, HERE I COME!

Front and rear windshields have different angles

The door is now locked in securely at the top and bottom

# City vehicles

What vehicles will your metropolis need? How about an ambulance for a hospital (see pages 58–59) or a scooter to help people zip around town? You could make a bike taxi for anyone who doesn't like to cycle themselves.

**AMBULANCE**

**WHAT'S NEXT?**

Start your model with a basic chassis made from some plates and spinning wheels. Where you go from there is up to you!

## Ambulance

When your citizens are feeling poorly, the speedy ambulance is ready to whisk them off to the city hospital. Leave space inside for the patient and lots of medical equipment.

White with red accents is a recognizable color scheme for medical treatment

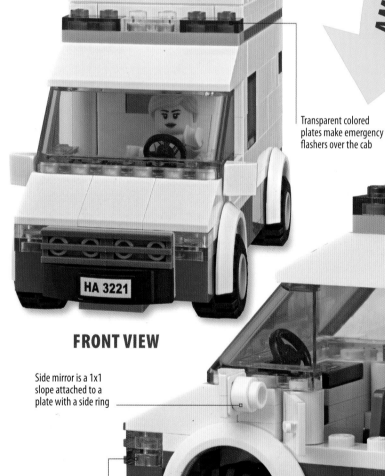

Transparent colored plates make emergency flashers over the cab

**FRONT VIEW**

Side mirror is a 1x1 slope attached to a plate with a side ring

Headlights and taillights are 1x1 plates built directly into the vehicle

*WE'LL HAVE YOU FEELING BETTER SOON.*

# SCOOTER

## Scooter

Cities have more than automobiles. A three-wheeled scooter is a fun way to get around without getting stuck in traffic. This one's front wheel is an airplane's landing gear.

With their tiny bumps and notches, click hinges are great for creating angles and articulation in small, lightweight models.

Handlebars are attached to a 1x1 plate with clip on top

Canopy shaped with half-arch pieces

A 1x1 plate with clip connects the stud on the back of the bike to a 1x2 plate with a hook-shaped bar on the passenger carriage

# BIKE TAXI

## Bike taxi

Running late for an appointment? Flag down a bike taxi for a pedal-powered trip through the city. You'll need a LEGO bicycle to start, but you can build the rest yourself.

Keep the bike and carriage level for a smooth ride

A plate with side rail provides a grip to lift off the roof

Transparent 1x1 round tiles create a row of bright floodlights above the rear door

Printed 1x1 tiles let medics monitor the patient's vital signs

A hinged door swings up out of the way

A clip can hold medical tools

Leave clearance so the stretcher can slide without bumping

Rear bumper is built on an 1x2/2x2 angle plate

**INSIDE VIEW**

HA 3221

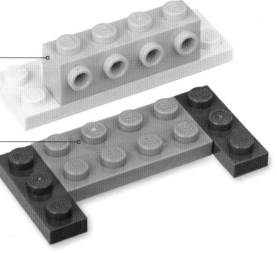

You could also use two 1x2 or four 1x1 bricks with side studs

These three plates are held together by the bigger plate on top

# Auto bumpers

Believe it or not, bumpers can be the hardest part of a car or truck model to build. Try using these techniques to make your own detailed and good-looking auto bumpers.

## 1 Basic structure

Start by placing a 1x4 brick with side studs on a 2x6 plate with the studs pointing out. Add an under-layer made from a 2x4 plate and two 1x3 plates.

Attach two 1x2 LEGO grilles to a 1x4 plate

## 2 Build the details

The face of the bumper is built on a 2x4 plate. Assemble a grille for the top half, and a license plate area with side-lights for the bottom half.

JC60002

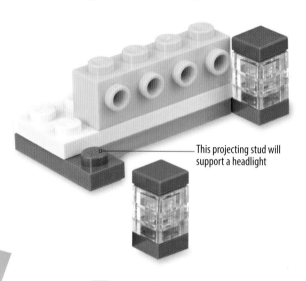

This projecting stud will support a headlight

## 3 Put it together

Make headlights by stacking up three transparent 1x1 plates with a 1x1 tile on top. Attach these on the sides. Next, connect the face to the side-stud brick to complete the bumper.

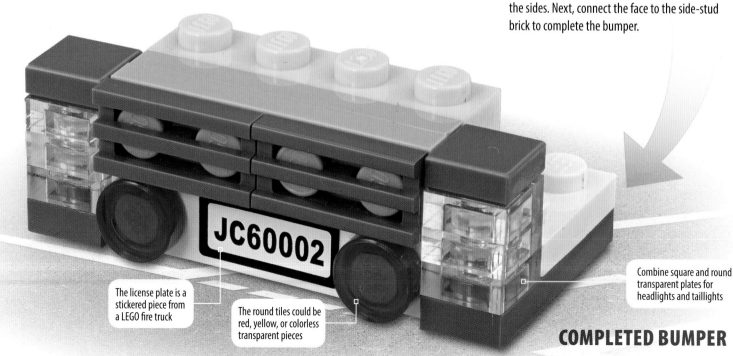

JC60002

The license plate is a stickered piece from a LEGO fire truck

The round tiles could be red, yellow, or colorless transparent pieces

Combine square and round transparent plates for headlights and taillights

**COMPLETED BUMPER**

## OTHER BUMPER IDEAS

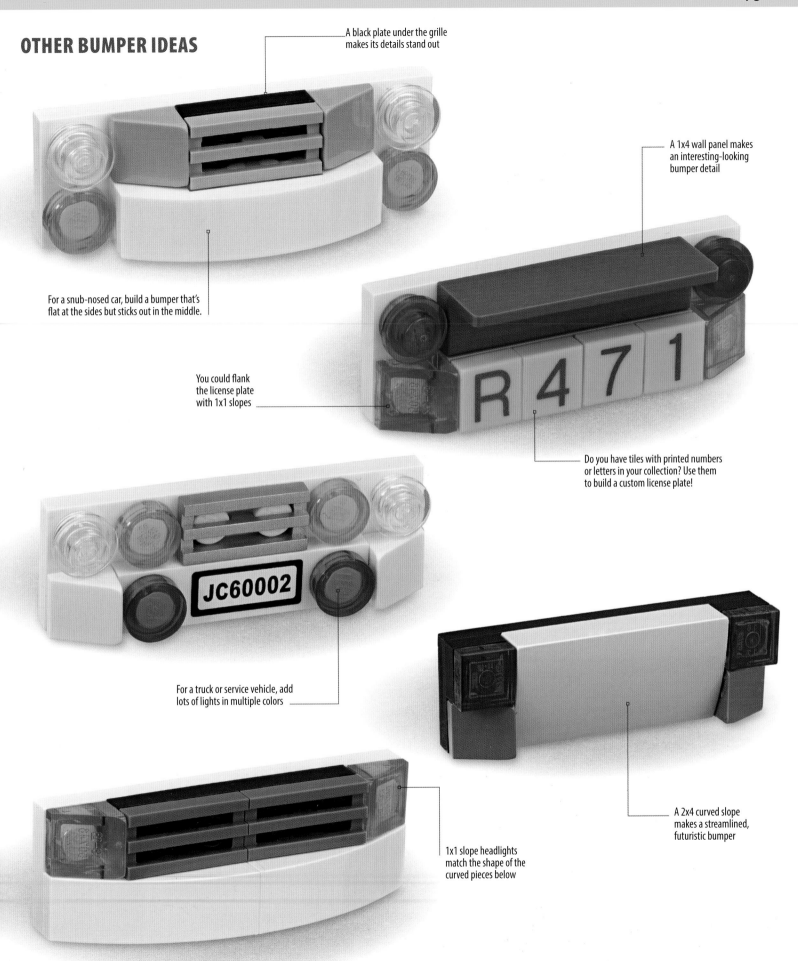

A black plate under the grille makes its details stand out

A 1x4 wall panel makes an interesting-looking bumper detail

For a snub-nosed car, build a bumper that's flat at the sides but sticks out in the middle.

You could flank the license plate with 1x1 slopes

Do you have tiles with printed numbers or letters in your collection? Use them to build a custom license plate!

For a truck or service vehicle, add lots of lights in multiple colors

A 2x4 curved slope makes a streamlined, futuristic bumper

1x1 slope headlights match the shape of the curved pieces below

# Lights, signs, and signals gallery

What else does a road system need? Build streetlights, traffic signals, directional signs, and other accessories to keep your city's traffic flowing smoothly.

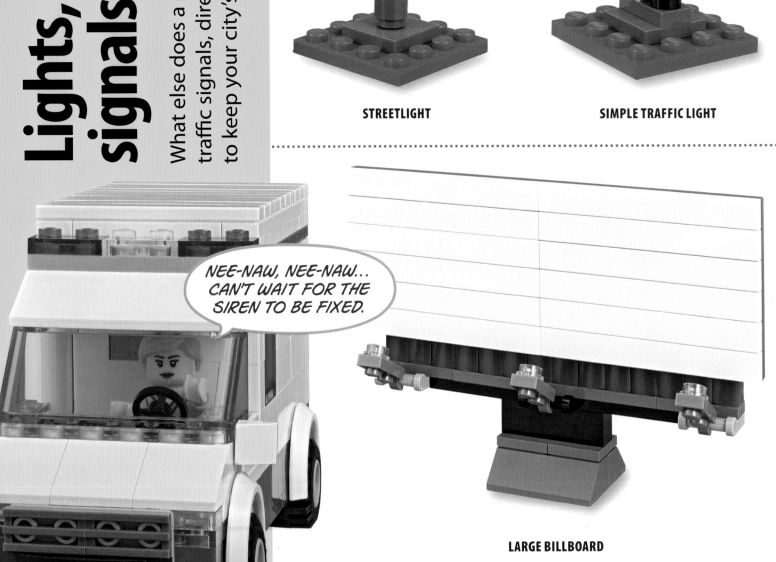

This useful bar-holder-with-clip element has a hole at one end and a clip at the other.

**STREETLIGHT**

**SIMPLE TRAFFIC LIGHT**

NEE-NAW, NEE-NAW... CAN'T WAIT FOR THE SIREN TO BE FIXED.

HA 3221

**LARGE BILLBOARD**

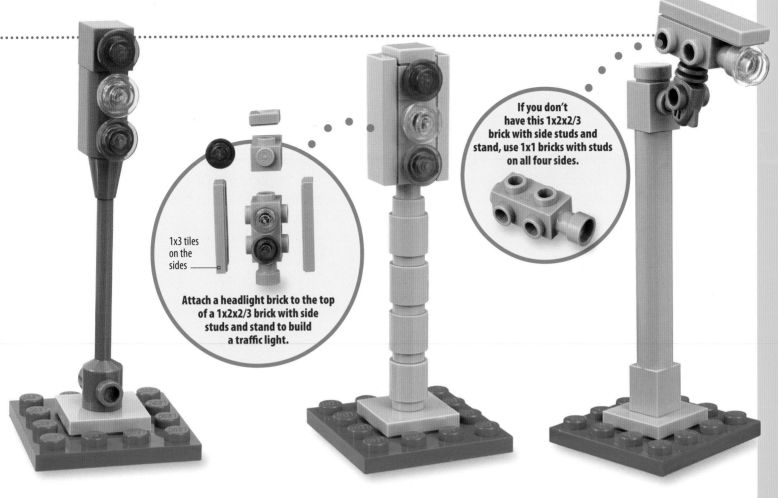

**1x3 tiles on the sides**

**Attach a headlight brick to the top of a 1x2x2/3 brick with side studs and stand to build a traffic light.**

If you don't have this 1x2x2/3 brick with side studs and stand, use 1x1 bricks with studs on all four sides.

**SIMPLE TRAFFIC LIGHT**

**ADVANCED TRAFFIC LIGHT**

**CLOSED-CIRCUIT CAMERA**

**SMALL BILLBOARD**

**BASIC SIGNS**

**STREET-CORNER SIGN**

**TRAFFIC SIGN**

# A farmer's field

With her road system complete, the city planner takes a drive to the countryside to see the sights around her modern metropolis. One of the first things she passes is a farmer plowing his field.

*IT'S A DIRTY JOB, BUT SOMEONE'S GOTTA DO IT!*

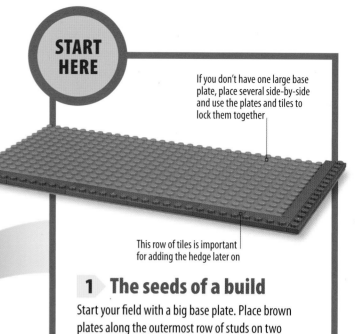

START HERE

If you don't have one large base plate, place several side-by-side and use the plates and tiles to lock them together

This row of tiles is important for adding the hedge later on

## 1   The seeds of a build

Start your field with a big base plate. Place brown plates along the outermost row of studs on two sides, and smooth tiles on the next row in.

## 2   Lay down some dirt

Cover part of the field with brown plates for freshly turned soil. Lay down long, thin plates over them to create the furrows where the farmer will plant his seeds.

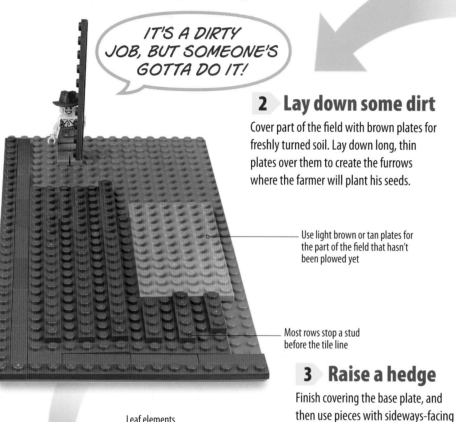

Use light brown or tan plates for the part of the field that hasn't been plowed yet

Most rows stop a stud before the tile line

## 3   Raise a hedge

Finish covering the base plate, and then use pieces with sideways-facing studs to build a tall hedge around two sides of the field. Make it look wild and untamed!

Leaf elements attached to plates

The field is now almost totally covered with "dirt"

Make an uneven pattern of 1x1, 1x2, 1x3, 1x4, and 2x3 plates

Stack multiple leaves in different directions for natural-looking plants

## Building the hedge

Start the hedge with a long, two-stud-wide green plate. Add smaller plates at different heights and levels to create natural-looking plant growth. If you have leaf pieces, use them too!

**4** **Private property**

Make a gate to mark the entrance to your field and keep crop-hungry creatures outside. Give it sturdy side posts and a clip-and-bar connection so that it can swing open and closed.

*TEE HEE.*

*THIS GATE KEEPS OUT THE RABBITS.*

Clips attach to 1x1 bricks with vertical bars

2x2 plate

**Use two 1x2 plates or one 2x2 plate to raise the post so the gate doesn't bump into studs on the base when it opens.**

Use ridged roof corner slopes for pointed tops

Turned sideways, this ladder becomes a gate

*A FARMER'S WORK IS NEVER DONE.*

**5** **It's plowing time!**

This field is only half-plowed, so the farmer still has lots to do. Put his tractor on the tan plates at the edge of the plowed section and watch him go!

**See more of this tractor and plow attachment on page 84.**

With the
here, it
is in t

# Crops and vegetables

Once the farmer's field is plowed, it's time to plant some crops. You can create all kinds of growing vegetables using your LEGO pieces. Since crops are planted in matching rows, pick out multiple parts with similar shapes and colors to create your growing plants.

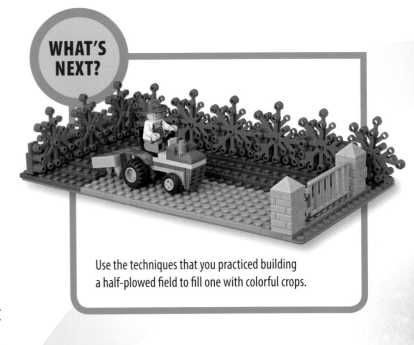

**WHAT'S NEXT?**

Use the techniques that you practiced building a half-plowed field to fill one with colorful crops.

**CARROTS**

## Carrots

To build this carrot field, start with a base made from one or more big plates. Add a second layer of two-stud-wide plates on top, with gaps between them to create the furrows where the carrots are planted. For an extra challenge, in some rows build carrots that have been growing for longer.

*THE ONES IN THE BACK LOOK READY FOR MY STEW.*

This row has a second orange round plate

The smallest carrots are made with one orange 1x1 round plate, and a green 1x1 flower plate for the leaves

## Cabbages

Leafy vegetables such as cabbages may look hard to build, but here's a fun and simple trick: arrange a few small plates at different levels, and then cover them with 1x1 slopes pointing in different directions. Hey presto—you've made a bunch of cabbages!

CABBAGES

PEOPLE WILL DIG MY CABBAGES.

Use brown, orange, or yellow plates to build dirt-covered fields

Cabbages are built in gaps in the top plate layer so they appear embedded in the ground

A green base creates a grassy country environment

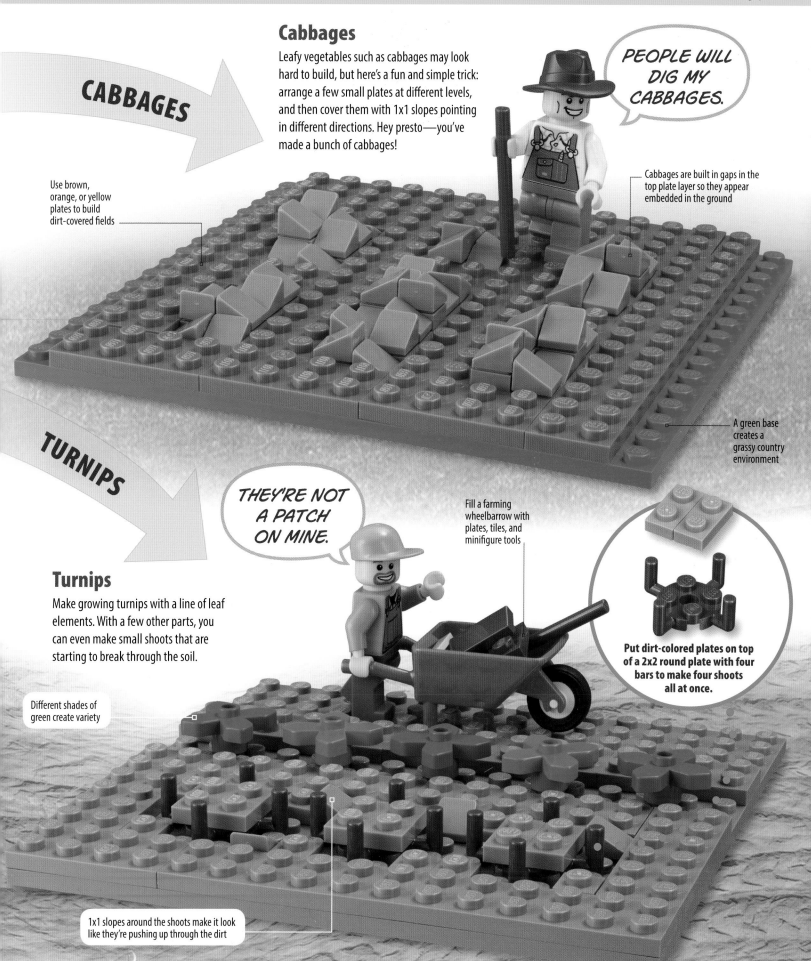

TURNIPS

THEY'RE NOT A PATCH ON MINE.

## Turnips

Make growing turnips with a line of leaf elements. With a few other parts, you can even make small shoots that are starting to break through the soil.

Fill a farming wheelbarrow with plates, tiles, and minifigure tools

Put dirt-colored plates on top of a 2x2 round plate with four bars to make four shoots all at once.

Different shades of green create variety

1x1 slopes around the shoots make it look like they're pushing up through the dirt

# Plants gallery

Bring your countryside to life with a colorful display of flowers and trees. Your choices of how to make them are almost unlimited, but here are some ideas to get your imagination going.

Layers of 2x2 round bricks and large plant leaves slot onto a bar piece to form this tree's foliage.

**SMALL TREE**

**BLOSSOM TREE**

**MEDIUM TREE**

*SHE'S BEEN IN THERE FOR HOURS, JUST STARING INTO SPACE.*

**GREENHOUSE**

LARGE TREE

APPLE TREE

FLOWER BED

SUNFLOWERS

# On the farm

The city planner stops by a farm to see how the farmers take care of their livestock. Try making some small farming scenes and vehicles. You can use official LEGO animals, or just build your own!

## Woolly sheep

This sheep has a lovely wool coat made by using lots of plates with side rings for the curls. Attach the head to a hinge brick and plate so the sheep can look up to check out where all the other sheep are going.

Use 1x1 plates with side rings and 1x2 grilles to make a woolly coat

1x2 hinged brick and hinged plate

Printed 1x1 round tiles for eyes

*DOES THIS MAKE ME A LAMB CHOP?*

A claw weapon doubles as a sheep-shearing tool

The sides of the pen are prison cell doors held on by clips on the base

## Sheep dip

Farmers sometimes dip their sheep to protect them from itchy bugs and disease. Use pieces with built-in bars to make fencing, and small transparent plates for the liquid in the dipping pool.

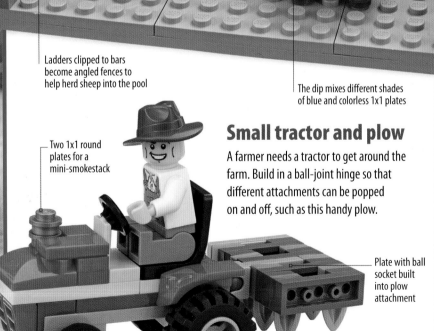

*OOH, IT'S TAKEN YEARS OFF ME.*

*C'MON FREDA, IT'S BATH TIME!*

Ladders clipped to bars become angled fences to help herd sheep into the pool

The dip mixes different shades of blue and colorless 1x1 plates

## Small tractor and plow

A farmer needs a tractor to get around the farm. Build in a ball-joint hinge so that different attachments can be popped on and off, such as this handy plow.

Two 1x1 round plates for a mini-smokestack

Plate with ball socket built into plow attachment

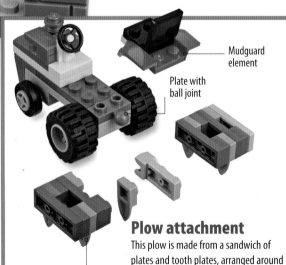

Mudguard element

Plate with ball joint

## Plow attachment

This plow is made from a sandwich of plates and tooth plates, arranged around a ball socket. Attach it using a ball joint built into the back of the tractor.

Tooth plates for plow teeth

# Country fair

At the country fair, all of the local farmers and craftspeople have put their best wares on display for the big judging competition. There's plenty of fresh and delicious food for sale, too!

## CARROT COMPETITION STALL

### Stall styles

The two fair stalls and their canopies have a similar shape, but are built very differently. The carrot contest stall is built straight up as shown, while the baker's market stall uses sideways building.

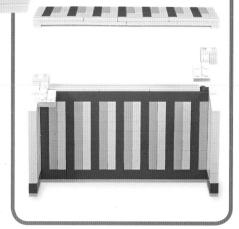

The judging table is made from plates, with a top of tiles and jumper plates

This colossal carrot is made from a 2x2 cone and a 2x2 dome, held together by a short LEGO Technic axle

A row of tooth plates creates a rippled canopy edge

## MARKET STALL

*JUST LAYING THE TABLE.*

**Use tiles of different shapes and colors to make a checkered tablecloth.**

# Leisure activities

It's been a long day, so the city planner decides to pitch a tent in a scenic spot and relax. Try building some outdoor leisure activities to give your minifigures a well-earned rest.

See how to build different kinds of trees on pages 82–83.

Use two half arches at different levels to create this shape of tree

Camping chairs are flag pieces fitted onto a 1x2 plate with a handled bar

Tent rests on 1x1 slopes under its sides

Backpack has two plates with handled bars

Guy ropes made from strings with studs and bars slotted into plates with clips, or use strings with studs at both ends

Small gray pieces for firepit ashes

Small camping table is a shield and a plate with clip on top of two silver round plates

## Campsite

The two-person tent (above) is built like the corner of a wall. There's an angled plate at the back and 1x1 slopes on two sides to keep it in position. The family tent (below) is made from three walls joined by hinges, with a fourth wall at the back. The support post in the middle attaches to side-stud bricks built into the top.

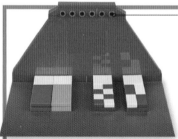

Row of side-stud bricks

## Supporting wall

A back wall will help support the three sides of the tent canopy. Use slopes to build it so that it matches the tent's shape. Side-stud bricks at the top connect to the canopy.

Build in clear bricks for a window

Flame pieces inserted into transparent cones make a toasty camping fire

*IT'S GREAT, BUT WHERE'S THE TV?*

Mushroom is a decorated radar dish on a 1x1 cone

The interior is spacious enough for the whole family

Use large tiles to make a smooth tarp under the tent

## Picnic area

Build some simple wooden tables and benches beneath a shady tree for a charming and scenic country picnic. Don't forget to pack some food, drinks, and accessories for some fun activities.

Thermos is a cup on top of a clear minifigure head element

*SOMETIMES LIFE REALLY IS A PICNIC.*

Make a juice carton with a 1x1 slope on a 1x1 brick

The benches are stacks of two brown one-stud-wide plates

You may need more than one tennis racket for a game!

Picnic table legs are made with log bricks and textured bricks

## Fishing

Build a sandy bank by a stream and set up your minifigures for a tranquil day of fishing. What a delightful way to while away a sunny country afternoon!

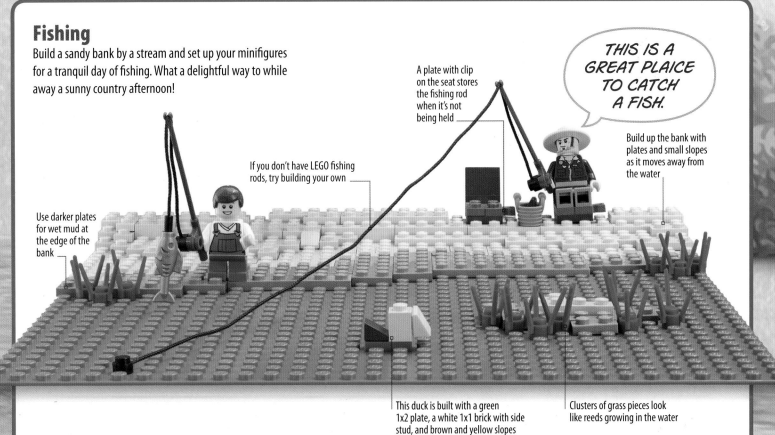

*THIS IS A GREAT PLAICE TO CATCH A FISH.*

A plate with clip on the seat stores the fishing rod when it's not being held

If you don't have LEGO fishing rods, try building your own

Build up the bank with plates and small slopes as it moves away from the water

Use darker plates for wet mud at the edge of the bank

This duck is built with a green 1x2 plate, a white 1x1 brick with side stud, and brown and yellow slopes

Clusters of grass pieces look like reeds growing in the water

## Modular building

It seems a long way from the basic building at the beginning of this chapter (pages 54–55) to this three-story farmhouse, but this build actually uses the same modular framework.

# Farmhouse

Now that she has toured the countryside, the City Planner is ready to stretch her building skills. Her challenge: to create a house for a farming family who live far from the hustle and bustle of the big city.

1x1 round bricks for chimney pots

A flat-roofed dormer lets you build small windows into the attic

For a roof, you can use slopes, tiles, plates, or even bricks stepped like stairs

Interlocking textured bricks create detailed corners

Use clips, bars, and other long, thin pieces to make drainpipes

Create window panes by combining multiple small windows into one large one

*AH, THE SWEET SMELL OF FRESH MANURE.*

Strong "stone" foundation for the first row of bricks

Attach leaf elements to bricks with side studs built into the wall to make creeping ivy.

## Window blinds

To create Venetian window blinds, alternate long, thin tiles with 1x1 plates at the sides. Tan bricks make wooden blinds, while other colors look like painted blinds.

REAR VIEW

*I FIND IVY A BIT CREEPY.*

SIDE VIEW

*I NEVER GET THE BED TO MYSELF.*

You can look more closely at some of the furniture in this house on page 66.

Who knows what old stuff could be lurking in the attic?

Add some growing plants outside

Use a LEGO staircase element, build your own, or combine both like this!

Curved pieces and tiles are useful for creating chairs and sofas

The city planner's busy metropolis is complete.

ONE DAY ALL THIS COULD BE YOURS!

BAA!

I ONLY CARRY PLASTIC.

I THOUGHT YOU WERE AN ICE-CREAM VAN!

# THE WILD WEST

Howdy, pardners! A new sheriff has been appointed for the little frontier town of Build City. They say it's a town full of bandits, cattle rustlers, and desperados of all kinds. Saddle up, round up your bricks, and ride along with the sheriff and his deputy on their mission to put together some of the rootin'est, tootin'est models in the whole wide Wild West. Yeehaw!

# A wagon

The sheriff and his deputy are ready to bring law and order to Build City, but they need a way to transport their supplies across the desert—and that means they need a wagon! First, find some flat rectangular plates to make the base. Brown and black pieces are the best because they look most like wood.

**START HERE**

LEGO® Technic pin connects to a wheel

6x10 plate

## 1 ▶ Build the platform

At its core, a wagon is a platform on wheels. Start with a bigger plate that's the size you want your wagon to be. Add connection points for wheels, and use a few smaller plates to lock them in place.

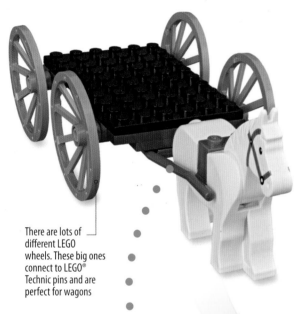

There are lots of different LEGO wheels. These big ones connect to LEGO® Technic pins and are perfect for wagons

## 2 ▶ Wheel position

Use a harness to attach a horse to your wagon's base. Then connect the wheels, adjusting their connection positions if the wagon sits too high or low. If your wagon keeps rolling away, then you can wait to put on the horse and wheels.

*I SURE HOPE THIS SEAT'S COMFORTABLE. WE'VE GOT A LONG RIDE AHEAD!*

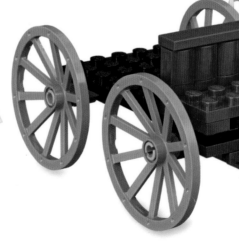

Studs on the seat give your minifigures something to attach to

Overlapping pieces make the wheel connections secure

For a smooth ride, it's important to make sure the height of your wagon matches the height of your horse's harness.

## 3 ▶ Take a seat

A 2x6 plate and two 1x2 plates create a short bench for the wagon driver. Stacked log bricks give the back-rest the appearance of being made out of wood.

YEP, GOT ALL THE PROVISIONS!

Make the side-planks uneven for an old-fashioned, rickety appearance

Keep the back of the wagon low to allow for loading and unloading

Place tiles on top of barrel and crate elements for lids

See page 99 to look more closely at these rock formations.

## 4 ▶ Load it up

The back of the wagon carries provisions and equipment. Build walls so they don't tumble out. Tiles attached to sideways-facing studs look like the wooden planks on the sides of a real Western wagon.

The deputy doesn't really use this whip—it's just for show

A cowboy hat keeps the sun off your face on a long desert ride

## 5 ▶ Roll out!

Great work, cowpoke! Don't forget to roll your wagon to make sure its wheels are even. Now that you've built a good and sturdy wagon, you're ready to hit the trail. But what sights will your Wild Western duo see along the way?

# Wagons roll

Your first wagon was fairly simple, but you might run into a few fancier types as you travel on the road. Each of these wagons started out the same way, but they were built up differently so they could be used for different jobs.

**WHAT'S NEXT?**

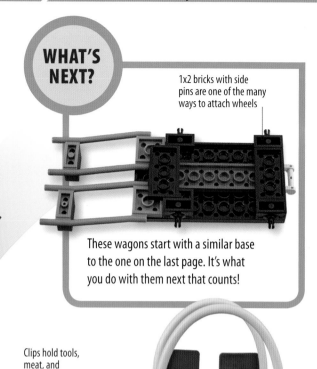

1x2 bricks with side pins are one of the many ways to attach wheels

These wagons start with a similar base to the one on the last page. It's what you do with them next that counts!

**CHUCK WAGON**

## Chuck wagon

This wagon transports fresh meat and produce to the nearby cavalry fort. It's similar to the earlier wagon model, but a little trickier because of the curved tubes that give it its shape.

Clips hold tools, meat, and bottles inside the wagon

**REAR VIEW**

Make a covered wagon by putting fabric over the tubes to shade the cargo

Flexible LEGO tube element bent into a curve

*EASY NOW, MY LITTLE BEAUTIES.*

Smaller wheels keep the wagon closer to the ground

This horse has an extra joint that lets it rear up on its hind legs—see it in action on page 100!

These wheels connect to an axle plate with attached pins

Hitch up two horses to pull heavier loads

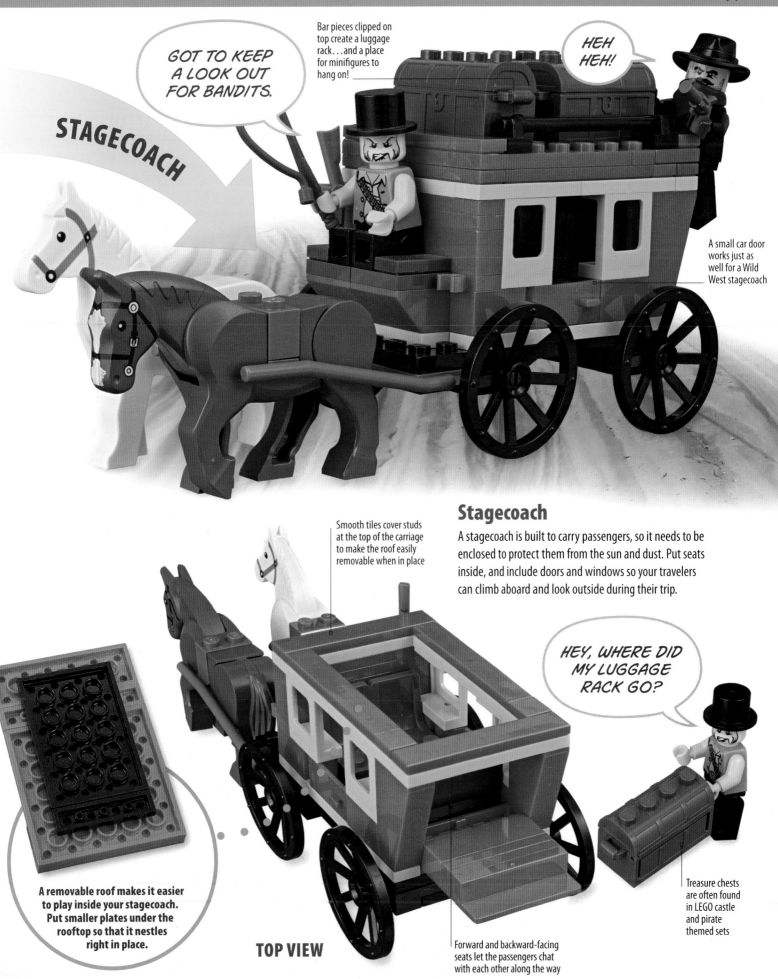

**STAGECOACH**

GOT TO KEEP A LOOK OUT FOR BANDITS.

Bar pieces clipped on top create a luggage rack...and a place for minifigures to hang on!

HEH HEH!

A small car door works just as well for a Wild West stagecoach

## Stagecoach

A stagecoach is built to carry passengers, so it needs to be enclosed to protect them from the sun and dust. Put seats inside, and include doors and windows so your travelers can climb aboard and look outside during their trip.

Smooth tiles cover studs at the top of the carriage to make the roof easily removable when in place

HEY, WHERE DID MY LUGGAGE RACK GO?

A removable roof makes it easier to play inside your stagecoach. Put smaller plates under the rooftop so that it nestles right in place.

**TOP VIEW**

Forward and backward-facing seats let the passengers chat with each other along the way

Treasure chests are often found in LEGO castle and pirate themed sets

# Western scenery

You might think there's little to see in the great, wide Western outdoors, but experienced range riders know that every lonely rock and plant just adds to the mystery of their surroundings. Fill your Wild West landscape with interesting scenery, just like this!

Headlight brick

Brown 2x2 round bricks and tiles look like carved wood

**Create faces with headlight bricks for eyes, slopes for beaks, and curved half arches for wings or antlers.**

## Totem poles

Accompanied by the sound of traditional drums, tall totem poles rise at the side of the river. When building village details, try looking at pictures of the real thing for reference.

Ridged roof slope

Stick to two or three colors on each pole

## Tribal drums

In a village in the desert, the chief beats out a rhythm on some traditional drums. This simple build uses a 2x2 round red brick for a base with a 2x2 round brown plate for decoration. Give it a smooth surface by using a 2x2 tile on the top.

Multiple plates look like raised, uneven ground

Flame pieces and turkey leg are plugged into the hollow studs of jumper plates

Build a checked bedroll with 1x1 tiles in two or more colors

## Round the campfire

It's getting dark, so the sheriff and deputy have built a campfire to cook a hearty supper, then they'll take turns snoozing on the bedroll until morning. They need some rest if they're going to catch an outlaw!

Rock spire tapers from a wide base to a pointy top

Different colored plates represent bands of different rock

A short LEGO Technic axle connects the trunk to the cross-shaped hole on a 2x2 round brick

Inverted slopes let you widen the spire midway up

This piece with four bars lets you attach the leaves.

## Desert landscape

It takes a special kind of tree to survive in the harsh desert climate. Angled LEGO Technic connector pieces give this hardy survivor a twisted trunk. A big, spiky cactus and an old cow skull are other familiar sights in the desert. Include these to make any Wild West scene recognizable and exciting.

A 1x1 green plate goes on top

Inside the cactus is a core of 1x1 bricks with studs on their tops and sides. These are spaced out by 1x1 round plates.

The arms are made with small plates and slope bricks

These pieces can be any color because they are hidden from view

CACTUS FOR DINNER TONIGHT!

Cow skull is made from a 1x1 brick, a 1x2 jumper plate, two 1x1 bricks with hollow side studs, and two horn pieces

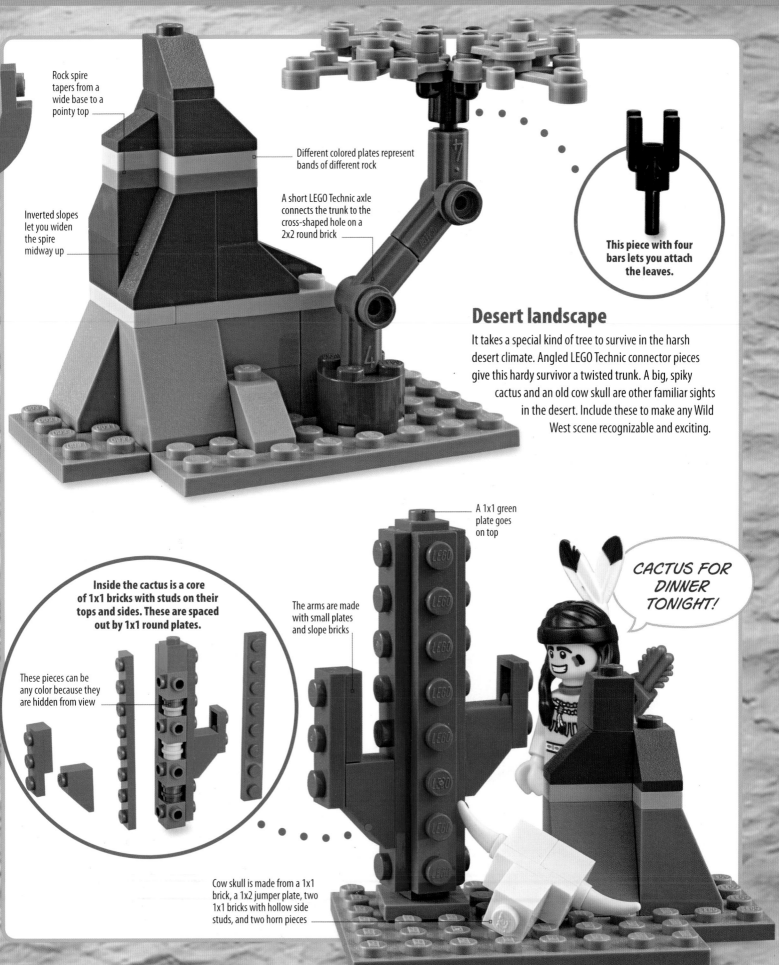

# Cavalry fort

The sheriff stops off at a remote cavalry fort, where the soldiers inform him that, rumor has it, a notorious outlaw is headed for Build City... Add life to your Wild West plains by building locations for your characters to visit while on the road.

> WHAT'S THAT RUSTLING SOUND?

> OOPS, SORRY. THAT'LL BE MY PACKET OF NUTS.

A low notch in the wall lets a cannon poke out

> THIS POSE TELLS EVERYONE I'M IN CHARGE.

Epaulettes go over the shoulders

A rearing steed provides a battle-ready action pose

The base of this cannon platform is built in a similar way to the wagon on page 94.

### Cavalry captain

A high-ranking cavalry soldier should look important. Give your fort's captain extra decorations and accessories so that everybody can tell he's in charge.

Use tan and dark tan plates for a sandy display base

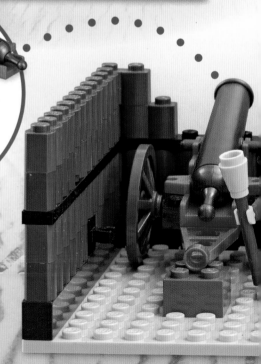

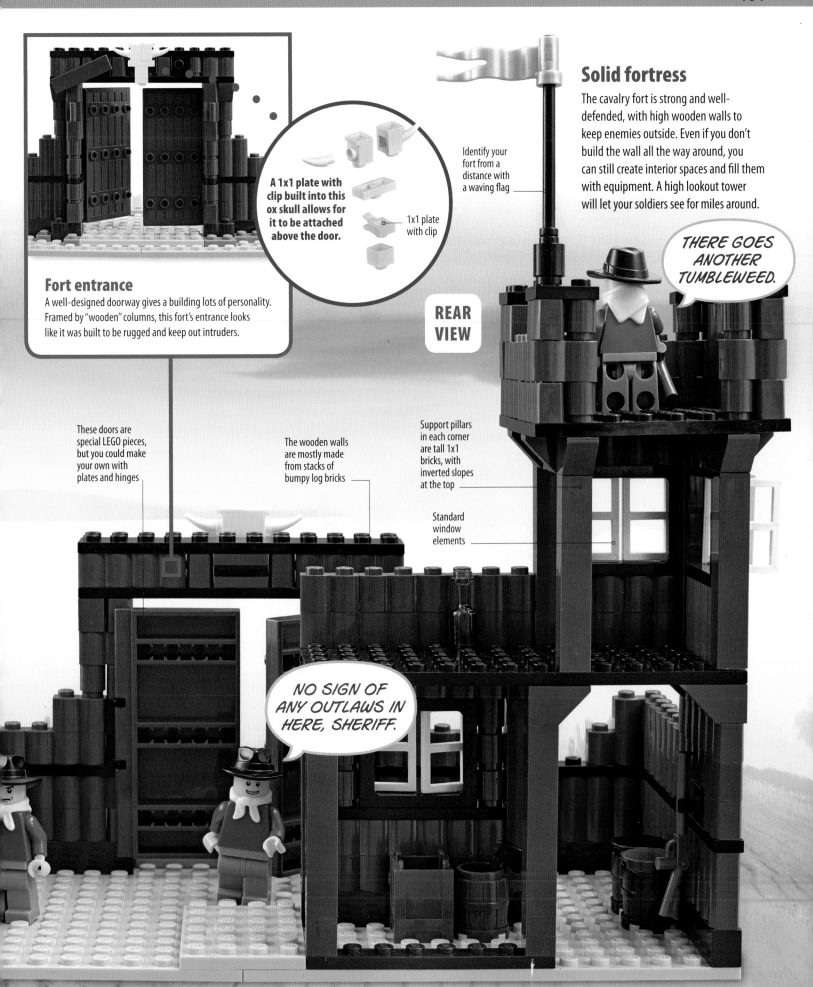

## Solid fortress

The cavalry fort is strong and well-defended, with high wooden walls to keep enemies outside. Even if you don't build the wall all the way around, you can still create interior spaces and fill them with equipment. A high lookout tower will let your soldiers see for miles around.

THERE GOES ANOTHER TUMBLEWEED.

Identify your fort from a distance with a waving flag

**A 1x1 plate with clip built into this ox skull allows for it to be attached above the door.**

1x1 plate with clip

## Fort entrance

A well-designed doorway gives a building lots of personality. Framed by "wooden" columns, this fort's entrance looks like it was built to be rugged and keep out intruders.

These doors are special LEGO pieces, but you could make your own with plates and hinges

The wooden walls are mostly made from stacks of bumpy log bricks

Support pillars in each corner are tall 1x1 bricks, with inverted slopes at the top

Standard window elements

REAR VIEW

NO SIGN OF ANY OUTLAWS IN HERE, SHERIFF.

# A jailhouse

The sheriff and his deputy have arrived in town to discover that the outlaw got there first—and busted one of his gang out of jail! Try building your own jailhouse for a no-good bandit to break out from.

**START HERE**

Tiles of different lengths, widths, and colors look like the boards have been broken and replaced over the years

Leave a gap in the foundation for the door

### 1 ▸ Ground work

Using a big tan base plate to represent the dusty ground, add a boardwalk for an old-fashioned path. A layer of dark gray bricks makes a stone foundation.

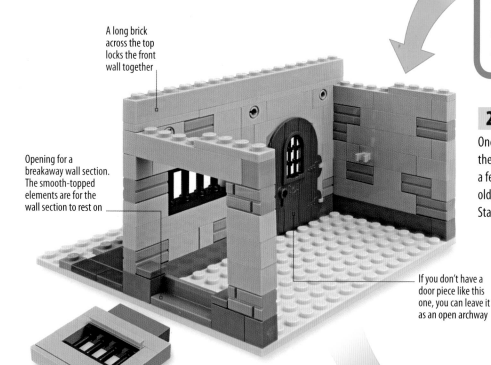

A long brick across the top locks the front wall together

Opening for a breakaway wall section. The smooth-topped elements are for the wall section to rest on

If you don't have a door piece like this one, you can leave it as an open archway

### 2 ▸ Build crumbling walls

Once your foundation is complete, you can build the walls and door. Mix regular LEGO bricks with a few textured elements to create walls that look old, with the plaster crumbling and falling off. Stagger the rows of bricks to make them stronger.

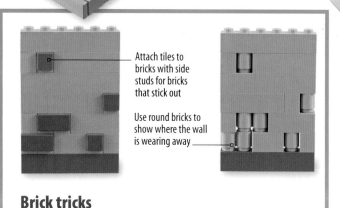

Attach tiles to bricks with side studs for bricks that stick out

Use round bricks to show where the wall is wearing away

#### Brick tricks

Here are some other ways to make weathered stone walls. The trick is to add texture instead of having a wall that looks totally smooth.

### 3 ▸ Outside jail

What features might you need outside the jail? In the Old West, people rode around on horseback, so how about a hitching post for them to tie their horses to while they go inside a building?

...JUST TAKING A LITTLE WALK...

Small dark tan plates look like piles of dirt or mud

A roof doesn't have to cover the entire buidling. Leaving some open space makes it easier to play inside

**COVER YOUR EARS AND COUNT TO FIVE.**

Smooth-topped elements will be a resting surface for breakaway wall

A central wall supports the long bricks of the roof's edge

Clips make a good place to store the sheriff's rifles

The sheriff will need some simple furniture to sit on while he waits for the next emergency

Wooden beam-ends are brown 1x1 round bricks attached to LEGO Technic pins plugged into bricks with holes in the wall.

Barred elements are good for making gates, fences, and prison windows

Hitching post is a bar held by wrenches pushed into stacks of 1x1 round bricks

### 4 In jail...for now

This isn't just the jailhouse—it's also the sheriff's office. Build a wall through the middle to divide the two halves, just make sure the front door is on the sheriff's side!

**I'M OUTTA HERE!**

**BOOM!!**

This bottom brick fits perfectly into the T-shaped base of the wall

### Walled in

The breakaway section fills the gap and makes the wall look like one solid build. By covering up the studs, you can keep them from sticking together.

# Around town

Build up the rest of your Wild West town, one building at a time. A bank and a general store might sit near the jailhouse, with a ranch right outside of town.

**WHAT'S NEXT?**

**BANK**

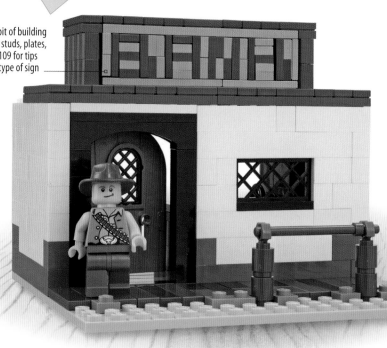

Use matching base plates and tile boardwalks to make all your buildings line up when placed side-by-side along a street.

## Bank

Give your townsfolk a place to store their coins and valuables by providing your town with a trusty bank. Just beware of bank robbers!

The sign is a complicated bit of building involving sideways-facing studs, plates, and tiles. See pages 108–109 for tips on how to make a similar type of sign

A layer of brown tiles makes a roof of wooden boards

Shiny tile floorboards give the bank a high-class atmosphere

**REAR VIEW**

## Western ranch

Use two base plates to make this ranch: one for the building, and the other for the next-door corral. Now you've got somewhere to keep your farm animals so they don't run loose through town!

C'MON BESSIE. JUMP THROUGH THE LOOP!

AIN'T GONNA HAPPEN.

A flower stem element can also be a small patch of grass

# GENERAL STORE

This ornament is made with a 1x1 cone and a 1x1 plate with vertical clip, snapped onto a plate with a bar in the sign's façade

**REAR VIEW**

Crates, barrels, and wall clips for displaying wares

## General store

You'll find everything you need for life in the Wild West at the local general store, from carrots to dynamite. Put a big sign on the roof so everybody knows where to shop.

Look closer at some of the Western town items on pages 110 and 111.

Include some friendly store staff

# WESTERN RANCH

Colorful tile roof sits on top of the ranch house at an angle

The fence boards are attached to bricks with side studs

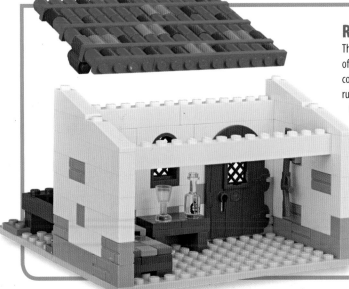

## Ranch roof

This roof is made from stacks of 1x1 round bricks in different colors, with rows of narrow plates running through for strength. It has log bricks built into it that face downward. They allow the roof to rest on a long brick that spans across the back of the ranch.

**REAR VIEW**

# Wild West saloon

A Wild West town wouldn't be nearly so wild without its saloon. From card games to cowboy brawls, there's always something going on inside. That's why it's the outlaw's favorite hangout when he isn't busy breaking the law!

WHAT'S NEXT?

SALOON

You've made single-story buildings, why not try adding two-story buildings to your Wild West town's street?

Look more closely at how this sign is built on pages 108–109.

## Outside the saloon

From the outside, you can see the saloon's famous double-swing doors, extra large windows, and wooden balcony. A big two-story building like this takes careful planning, so interlock your bricks securely to stop it coming apart.

Fill in the railing's gap with a stack of two 1x1 round bricks, held in place by a 1x3 plate

THIS IS JUST MY KINDA PLACE.

The balcony's support columns are built with tall 1x1 bricks, small arches, and 1x2 inverted slope bricks.

**The canopy ends attach to the tops of headlight bricks sticking out of the front wall.**

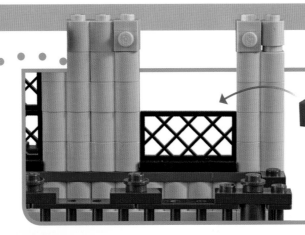

## Decorative window

The top half of the window is a latticed fence attached to an upside-down 1x4 brick with side-studs, which is plugged into the six-stud-long green canopy.

## Inside the saloon

The interior of the saloon has a bar with drinks, a space for customers to sit, and a second-floor balcony where minifigures can stand and watch the action below. What's going on downstairs is up to you!

Brown stripes are where the roof and balcony are built directly into the walls for strength

*I HAVEN'T SEEN SHAKESPEARE FOR SOME TIME.*

Use columns to support both the balcony and the roof

The interior railings match the exterior railings

Instead of a full second floor the upstairs has a curved railing

A curved railing makes a smooth transition to the wall

If you don't have these window shutters, you can build custom swing doors with plates and bars for hinges

*HE'S BARD!*

Add brass detailing by snapping a gold bar element into clips at the base of the bar

**REAR VIEW**

# Building signs

Every good Wild West store needs a big sign on top. There are lots of different ways to build signs with lettering out of LEGO bricks. Here are some examples—from simple to more challenging—to get you started.

## 1 Simple plate sign

This simpler sign is made by stacking plates sideways to spell out letters. Here's how you can build a letter "S" and a letter "A". Practice with your own pieces to make the rest of the alphabet.

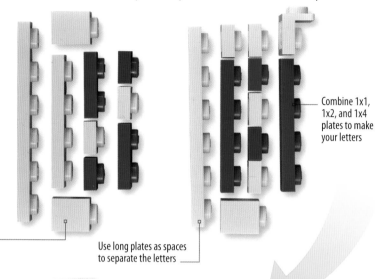

Combine 1x1, 1x2, and 1x4 plates to make your letters

Create a layer of 1x1 bricks above and below the letters

Use long plates as spaces to separate the letters

All these letters are made to be the same width—they are two or three plates wide

 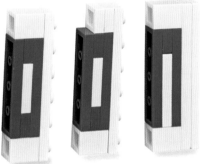

## 2 Full word

Once you've built the letters, put them together to make the complete word. Remember to include spaces between letters or your sign may be hard to read. You can build a brick with a side stud into the top edge to attach an arched detail above the sign.

Pick contrasting colors for the letters so they stand out

Arch attaches using 1x2 angle plates

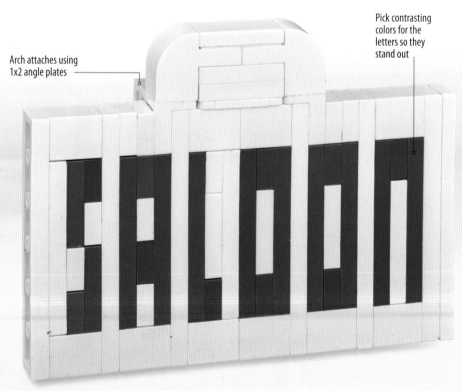

**COMPLETED SIMPLE SIGN**

# 1 ▶ Complex sign

Start with a background wall that includes bars attached to clip plates. Then build the vertical (upright) parts of each letter using sideways plates and tiles. Include a 1x1 plate with a horizontal clip in each part so it fits onto the bar.

Leave gaps the size of 1x2 bricks at the bottom of the back wall for the lower section to slot into

These vertical columns are built to fit between the horizontal ones shown below.

Use clips and bars fitted onto the sign's background wall

You can make most letters with 1x1 or 1x2 plates and bricks, but you'll need a 1x2 brick with hole for some of them.

Each segment is a 1x1 stack of plates (including a plate with a horizontal clip), with a tile on top

A 1x2 plate with 2 clips on a stack of two plates equals the shape of one 1x2 LEGO brick—so it will fit the gaps in the back wall perfectly

Long tiles on the base make the bottom border of the sign

# 2 ▶ Horizontal lines

Stack up the horizontal parts of the letters using 1x1 plates and tiles in a similar way, but using 1x1 plates with vertical clips instead of horizontal ones. Attach these bars to clips mounted on the sign's base.

# 3 ▶ Finish it off

Finally, slot the two sections together so that the vertical and horizontal segments line up. Build an arch and a roof on top with tiles, plates, and arch pieces.

Use tiles for a smooth top layer that hides the sign's inner workings!

Keep a few studs exposed for ornamentation

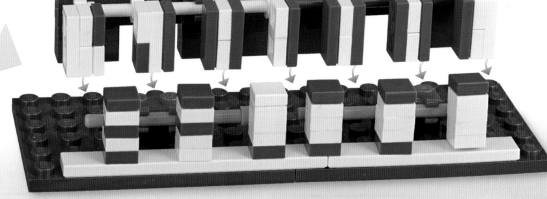

**COMPLETED COMPLEX SIGN**

# Town items gallery

To make your LEGO models feel like they come straight out of the Wild West, try including people, animals, furniture, and other mini-builds in your models to really set the scene.

**SALOON TABLES**

**WOODEN DOORS**

**DESK AND CHAIR**

SING ALONG IF YOU KNOW THIS ONE, FOLKS.

This piano has white grille pieces for the keys and a 1x1 slope for the foot pedal. Bricks with side studs hold up the sheet music.

**PIANO**

**BANK SAFE**

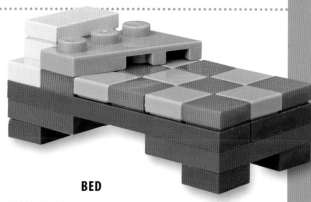

**SIDE TABLE OR BENCH**

**CRATE OF DYNAMITE**

**BARREL**

**BED**

**SWINGING DOORS**

**IRON LANTERN**

**BRASS LAMP**

**TABLE AND LAMP**

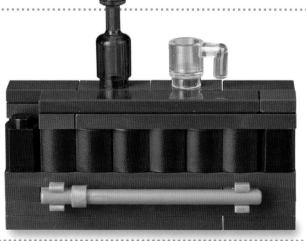

**BAR COUNTER**

**PIG PEN**

**WAGON HORSE**

**CAVALRY HORSE**

**WILD HORSE**

# A steam train

Every Wild West adventure could use a steam train. They're great for storing cargo, high-speed hold-ups, and chugging across the desert plains. Follow these steps to build a Western steam locomotive for yourself!

**START HERE**

A magnetic coupling in back connects to the next car

## 1 ▸ Undercarriage

Begin by using sturdy wheel bases from a LEGO train. The wheels are already spaced just right for LEGO train rails. If you don't have the parts, then you can make your own out of LEGO plates and wheels.

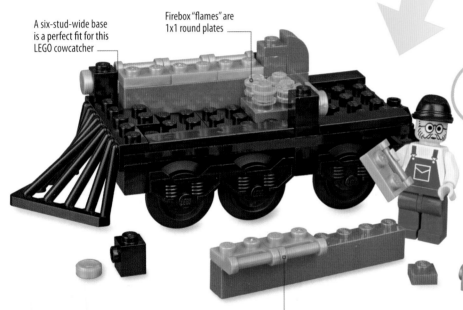

A six-stud-wide base is a perfect fit for this LEGO cowcatcher

Firebox "flames" are 1x1 round plates

*A FLASH OF GOLD MAKES HER LOOK REAL FANCY!*

## 2 ▸ Base and firebox

Use plates to connect the train wheels together and build the base out to its full width. Start building up the engine—use black for bare iron or bright colors for a fresh paint job. For a realistic detail, use transparent pieces to make a blaze inside the firebox to power the train.

Three gold 1x2 plates with handled bars in a row create a nice detail for the side of the locomotive

Use small half arches to create curved corners

A tile holds two small half arches together to make a smooth engine top

Black 1x1 round plate is attached to a jumper plate with a center stud

Tiles cover up the studs on the sides

## 3 ▸ A rounded engine

A locomotive's steam engine has a cylinder shape, so give it rounded corners if you have the right pieces. Along with decorative trim, place pieces with sideways studs at the front so you can attach forward-facing details.

If you don't have a special cowcatcher piece from a LEGO train, you can build your own out of slope and roof bricks

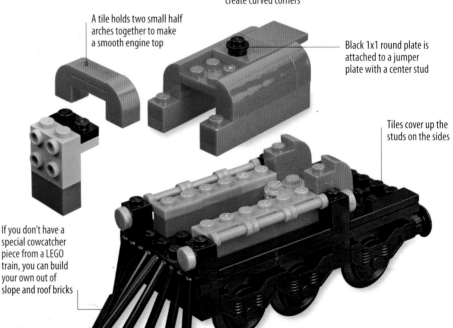

**The smokestack is a 4x4 cone attached upside-down with a LEGO Technic axle.**

## 4 ▶ Smokestack and cab

With the nose of the locomotive built, now make a cab in back where the engineer can drive and tend the firebox. Stack up 1x1 bricks to make the cab's corner supports, and add tile temperature controls. Don't forget a smokestack on top of the engine!

Plates with horizontal clips let you attach a pole for the engineer to hang onto

*JUST ONE MORE CAB CORNER TO GO!*

The train shares its color scheme with the riverboat (on pages 118–121) —maybe they are owned by the same company

Tiles with printed gauges and dials make this look like a mechanical engine

The roof is a 6x6 plate with 1x6 tiles on the sides

**Connect a stack of one radar dish and one 4x4 round plate to the side-stud pieces from Step 3 to make a round cap for the front of the engine.**

## 5 ▶ Wild West express

Add a roof to the engineer's cab, and your steam locomotive is done! Next, it's time to build the rest of the train. Turn the page to find out how!

# Train carriages

The outlaw has skipped town by hopping aboard the empty boxcar of a passing steam-powered train carriage. Use these train carriage ideas to inspire your own Western locomotives.

MINE CART

**WHAT'S NEXT?**

You've built the engine of a steam train. Now build some cars to pull behind it! If you don't have enough bricks, you could make a rolling mine cart instead.

Use a clear yellow 1x1 round plate for a light in front

Leave studs exposed for a rough, rocky appearance

## Mine cart

Gold miners use these carts to move gold ore from the heart of a mine to the entrance. Use a 2x6 plate for the base, and build up the front, back, and sides to create a hollow center for hauling cargo.

An angle plate attaches the headlight

1x4 bricks hold in the cargo

## Cart apart

Use inverted slopes at the front and back to give the cart its upside-down triangle shape. For the wheels, use auto wheel hubs without their tires, snapped onto a 2x2 plate with small axle pins.

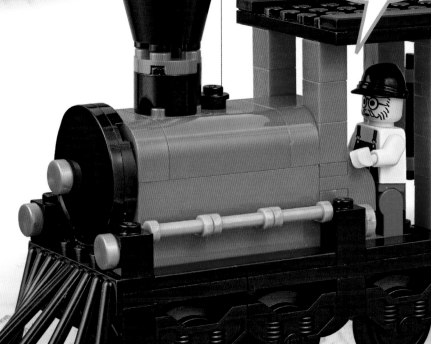

Train whistle is a 1x1 round plate attached to a jumper plate

*MY FAVORITE PART IS WHEN THE WHISTLE GOES WOO-WOO!*

## COAL TENDER

### Coal tender

This small car with three walls is the coal tender, where the fuel for the steam engine is kept. Its open front end lets the engineer shovel coal into the firebox whenever it runs low.

"Coal" is a stack of black bricks with an uneven layer of 1x1 round plates on top

A plate with a clip holds the shovel in place

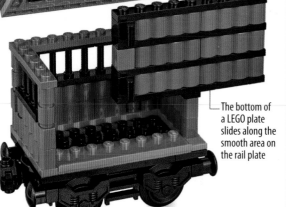

The studs on top slide through the groove on the plates bottom

Black stripe is formed by plates near the top of the coal pile

The bottom of a LEGO plate slides along the smooth area on the rail plate

If you don't have these magnetic couplings, then invent your own train car connections!

### Sliding door

Above and below the boxcar door are plates with side rails. Sandwiching the door between two of these plates lets it slide back and forth without falling off.

## BOXCAR

### Boxcar

Like many Western models, the boxcar uses brown log bricks together with round 1x1 bricks to create the appearance of wooden logs. Its sliding door is good for hauling important cargo...or hiding fugitives from the law.

MY FAVORITE PART IS WHEN I GET AWAY! HEH HEH HEH...

# The old mine

The outlaw's train ride leads to an old gold mine out in the desert. The same rock-building techniques used for the scenery on pages 98–99 can be used to make a mine entrance and an underground interior, where the sheriff is about to catch up with his most-wanted man.

## Mine entrance

Build a mine entrance just like you would a rock spire (see page 99), but add signs of labor such as a mine cart and rails, tunnel supports, and a cave-like archway leading into the mine.

Connect inverted slopes to other pieces around them for stability—you don't want your tunnel's roof to collapse!

Bricks with side studs built into the rocks will let you attach extra details

Make a strong base on both sides where you will build up the tunnel archway

Mixing dark and light brown creates an aged, weathered effect

Old carriage rails made from gray tiles and small brown plates

Use inverted slopes to build the sides of the tunnel toward each other at the top

A clip-mounted lantern lets miners see inside the dark tunnel

**Combine the mine ramp and desert scenery from pages 98–99 with the mine entrance to make an even more interesting scene.**

Add the mine cart from the previous page to build up your working scene

Little details like gold nuggets and tool crates add realism

*I'M STARTING TO FEEL A LITTLE BOULDER.*

**REAR VIEW**

# Inside the mine

The mine interior is built as a large backdrop. A high scaffold and a barrel held up by a chain give you ways for your minifigures to have a big, exciting action scene inside. Keep most of the model's weight near its base so that it won't tip over. Use inverted slopes to support the overhanging roof, but don't make it overhang too much or the mine wall may become unbalanced.

Outdoor scenery on top makes it look like the rest of the model is underground

Thin but natural-looking struts support the roof without making the top of the model too heavy

For the best balance, don't make the top wider than the base

STOP RIGHT THERE, TROUBLE MAKERS.

YOU WON'T CATCH ME, SHERIFF!

LUCKY I'M WEARING MY PLASTIC HAT!

Single-stud connection lets the barrel arm rotate or get knocked down in the fight. Fill the barrel with brick "rocks" or metal ore

A chain can just dangle to look like old equipment, or you could attach something to it, like a tool or even a prisoner

This iron lamp is similar to the ones on the riverboat (page 119), but with a small radar dish as a cover

# Rolling riverboat

The outlaw has fled the mine and is headed upriver! He has hopped aboard this paddlesteamer, with the sheriff in hot pursuit. Here are some pointers to help you build your own Wild West riverboat.

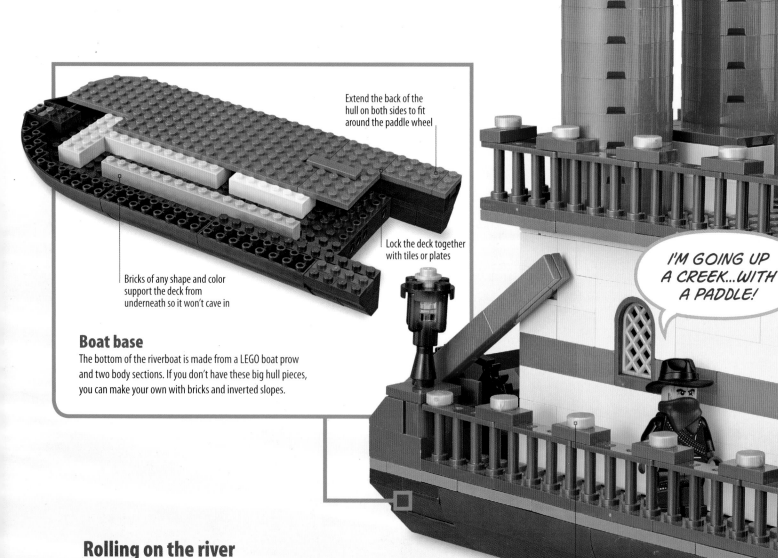

Extend the back of the hull on both sides to fit around the paddle wheel

Lock the deck together with tiles or plates

Bricks of any shape and color support the deck from underneath so it won't cave in

I'M GOING UP A CREEK...WITH A PADDLE!

## Boat base
The bottom of the riverboat is made from a LEGO boat prow and two body sections. If you don't have these big hull pieces, you can make your own with bricks and inverted slopes.

Gold details add a touch of wealth and luxury

## Rolling on the river
A Mississippi-style paddle steamer is a tough build, but it looks great when it's all assembled. Use colorful pieces to create a bright paint scheme, and as always for the Old West, include lots of brown wooden parts.

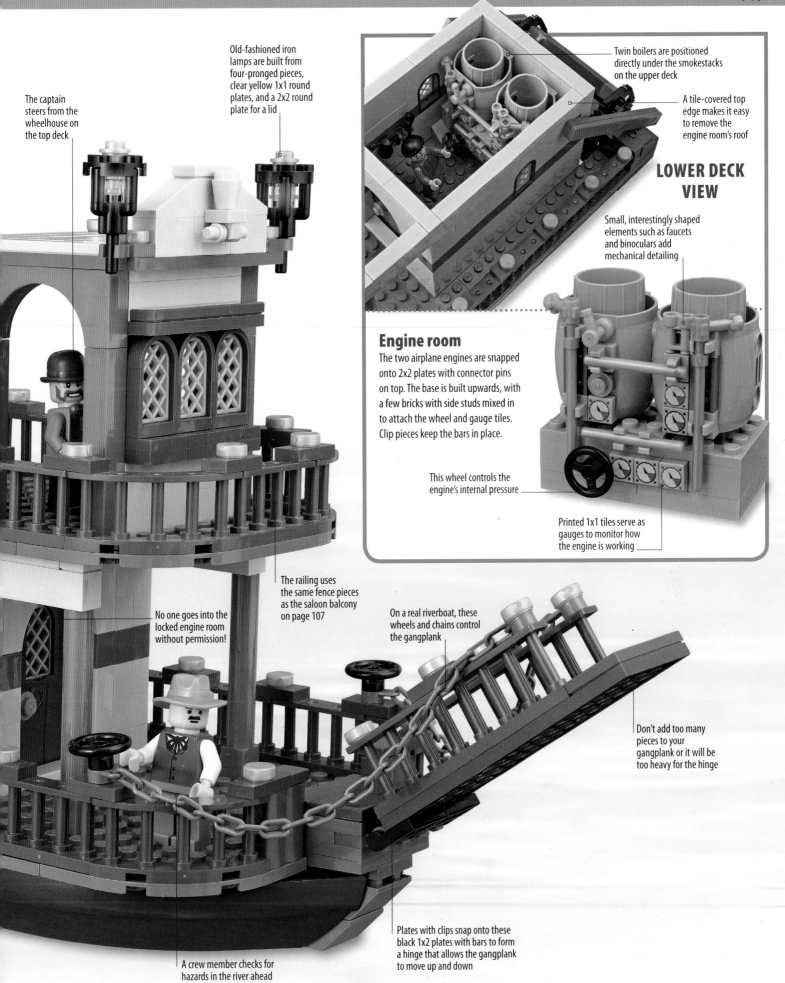

The captain steers from the wheelhouse on the top deck

Old-fashioned iron lamps are built from four-pronged pieces, clear yellow 1x1 round plates, and a 2x2 round plate for a lid

Twin boilers are positioned directly under the smokestacks on the upper deck

A tile-covered top edge makes it easy to remove the engine room's roof

## LOWER DECK VIEW

Small, interestingly shaped elements such as faucets and binoculars add mechanical detailing

## Engine room

The two airplane engines are snapped onto 2x2 plates with connector pins on top. The base is built upwards, with a few bricks with side studs mixed in to attach the wheel and gauge tiles. Clip pieces keep the bars in place.

This wheel controls the engine's internal pressure

Printed 1x1 tiles serve as gauges to monitor how the engine is working

The railing uses the same fence pieces as the saloon balcony on page 107

No one goes into the locked engine room without permission!

On a real riverboat, these wheels and chains control the gangplank

Don't add too many pieces to your gangplank or it will be too heavy for the hinge

A crew member checks for hazards in the river ahead

Plates with clips snap onto these black 1x2 plates with bars to form a hinge that allows the gangplank to move up and down

# Rolling riverboat (continued)

## Paddle wheel

The paddle wheel is built from tall and short 1x1 bricks, held together between two big hexagonal plates. A long LEGO Technic axle goes through the middle, with its ends held by bricks with holes on the back of the ship.

1x1 plates with clips hold lamps so other vessels can see the riverboat at night

A short wall separates the chimney-like smokestacks

*FULL STEAM AHEAD.*

## Rear paddle

A riverboat is propelled through the water by its rear paddle wheel, powered by steam generated by the engine. A rotating paddle wheel is the most important part of a riverboat model. Without one, it's just a boat!

Rear lamps have cones at their bases that attach to jumper plates

**REAR VIEW**

Gold 1x1 round tiles also make great Wild West coins

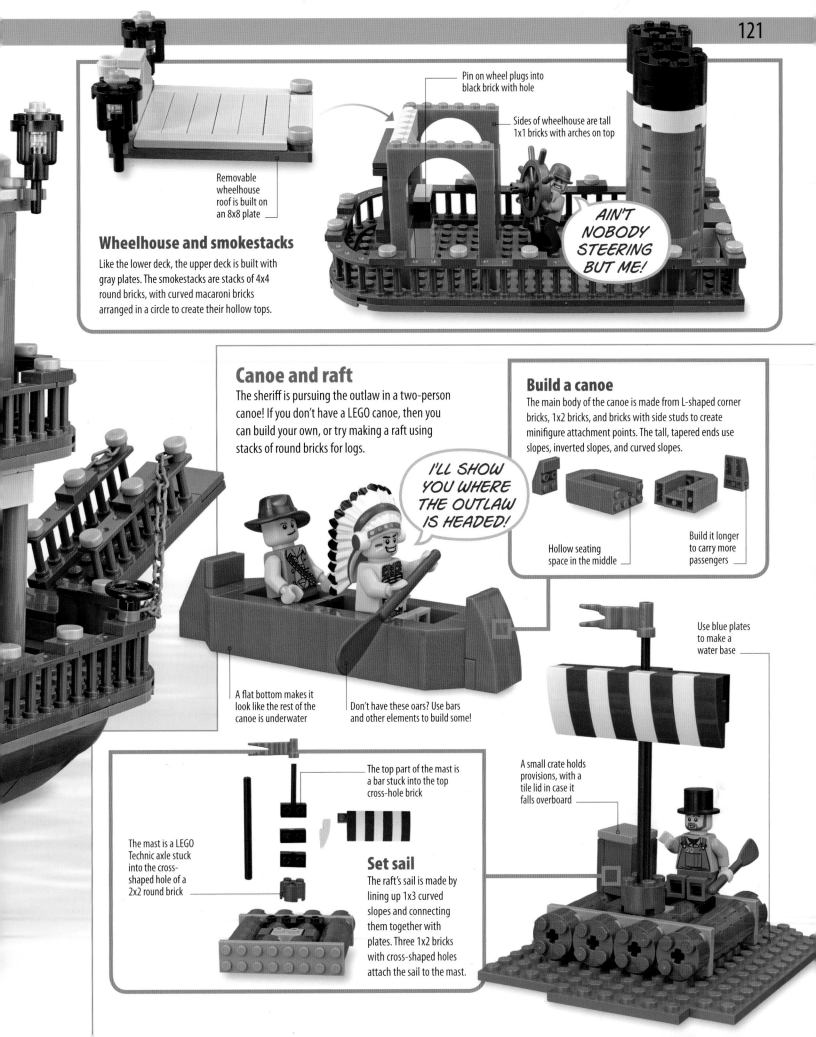

## Wheelhouse and smokestacks

Like the lower deck, the upper deck is built with gray plates. The smokestacks are stacks of 4x4 round bricks, with curved macaroni bricks arranged in a circle to create their hollow tops.

Removable wheelhouse roof is built on an 8x8 plate

Pin on wheel plugs into black brick with hole

Sides of wheelhouse are tall 1x1 bricks with arches on top

AIN'T NOBODY STEERING BUT ME!

## Canoe and raft

The sheriff is pursuing the outlaw in a two-person canoe! If you don't have a LEGO canoe, then you can build your own, or try making a raft using stacks of round bricks for logs.

I'LL SHOW YOU WHERE THE OUTLAW IS HEADED!

## Build a canoe

The main body of the canoe is made from L-shaped corner bricks, 1x2 bricks, and bricks with side studs to create minifigure attachment points. The tall, tapered ends use slopes, inverted slopes, and curved slopes.

Hollow seating space in the middle

Build it longer to carry more passengers

A flat bottom makes it look like the rest of the canoe is underwater

Don't have these oars? Use bars and other elements to build some!

Use blue plates to make a water base

A small crate holds provisions, with a tile lid in case it falls overboard

The mast is a LEGO Technic axle stuck into the cross-shaped hole of a 2x2 round brick

The top part of the mast is a bar stuck into the top cross-hole brick

## Set sail

The raft's sail is made by lining up 1x3 curved slopes and connecting them together with plates. Three 1x2 bricks with cross-shaped holes attach the sail to the mast.

# Outlaw hideout

The sheriff has found where the outlaw is keeping his ill-gotten loot—stashed inside a riverbank hideout! Create a scene that has two levels—just like the rugged mine on pages 116–117.

The duck's beak and wings are 1x1 tooth plates

**ROCKY ISLAND**

Like the desert scenery (page 99), using small and irregular plates as bases will let you move your river models around

These little plants are carrot tops stuck into the tops of 1x1 round bricks

## A simple riverbank

...or is it? This looks like an ordinary riverbank with a tree, flowers, and a small waterfall, but there's a surprise on the other side. When building a riverbank, try adding smaller rocky islands for a larger scene.

Rock face is made from large LEGO rock walls, with matching gray bricks and slopes built up on top

Gray 1x1 round plates for small rocks and pebbles

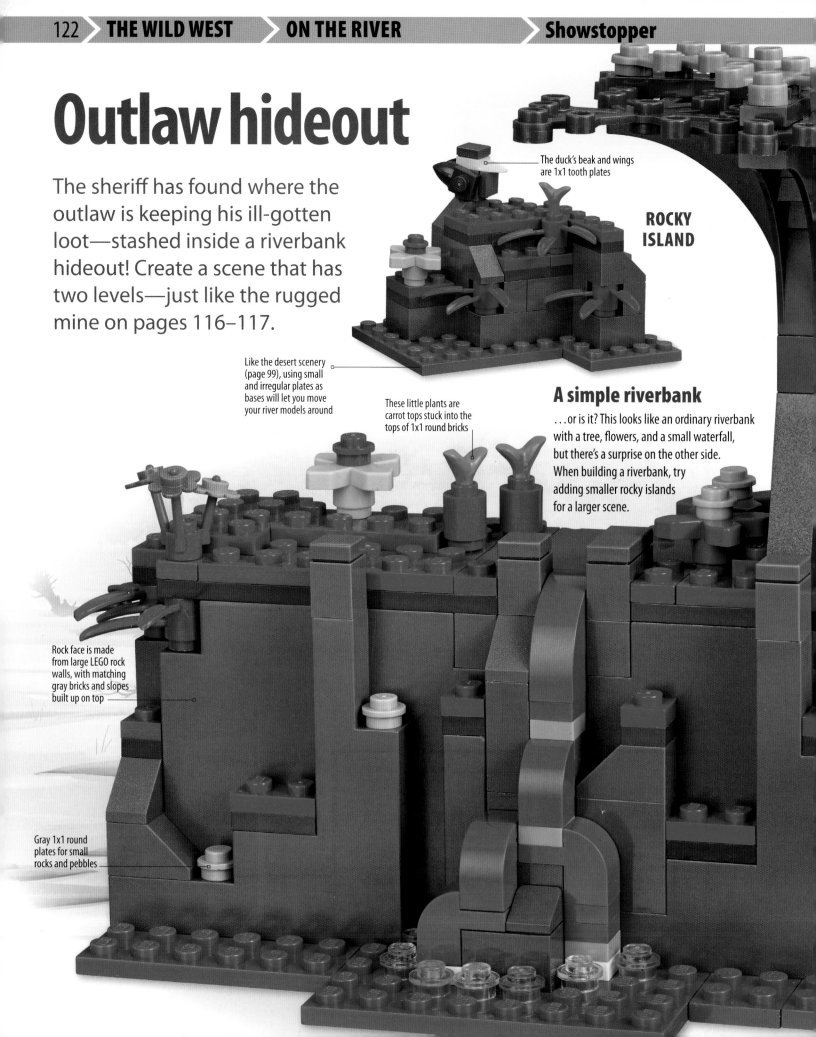

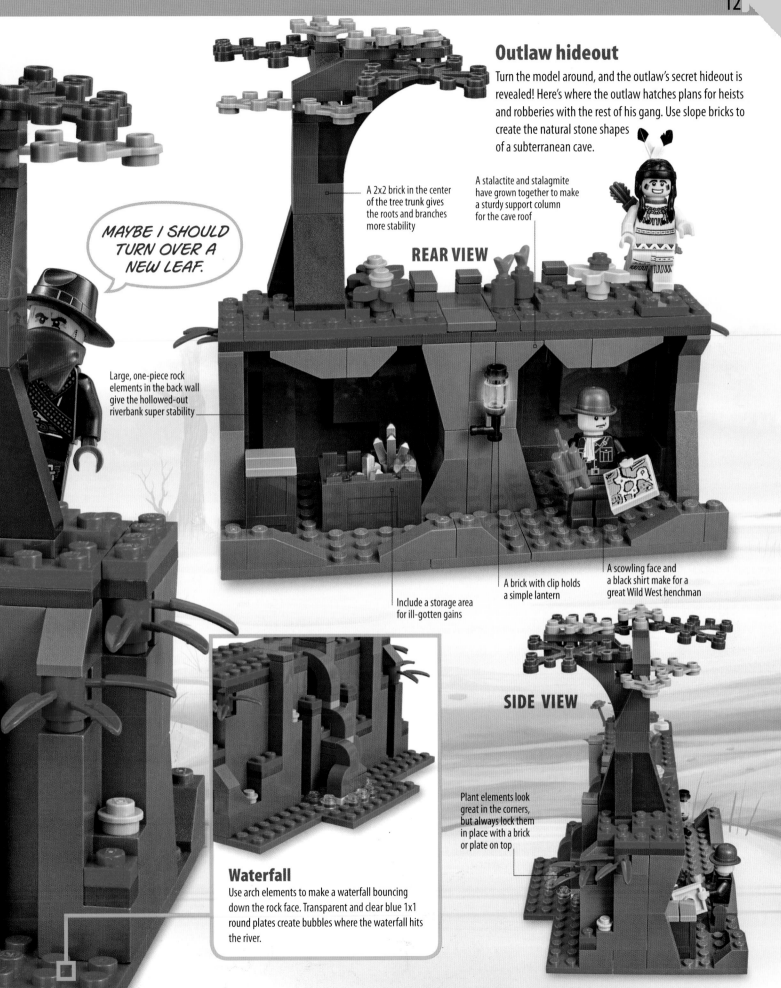

## Outlaw hideout

Turn the model around, and the outlaw's secret hideout is revealed! Here's where the outlaw hatches plans for heists and robberies with the rest of his gang. Use slope bricks to create the natural stone shapes of a subterranean cave.

A 2x2 brick in the center of the tree trunk gives the roots and branches more stability

A stalactite and stalagmite have grown together to make a sturdy support column for the cave roof

**REAR VIEW**

*MAYBE I SHOULD TURN OVER A NEW LEAF.*

Large, one-piece rock elements in the back wall give the hollowed-out riverbank super stability

Include a storage area for ill-gotten gains

A brick with clip holds a simple lantern

A scowling face and a black shirt make for a great Wild West henchman

**SIDE VIEW**

Plant elements look great in the corners, but always lock them in place with a brick or plate on top

## Waterfall

Use arch elements to make a waterfall bouncing down the rock face. Transparent and clear blue 1x1 round plates create bubbles where the waterfall hits the river.

Order is restored in Build City—or is it?

MORE TUMBLEWEED...

SAL[OON]

[S]tore

BANK

WE'VE GOT ANOTHER PROBLEM, SHERIFF.

MAKE THAT TWO! YIKES.

# Fantasy Land

Meet Alice. No, not that Alice! This Alice is just an ordinary girl who likes to escape her everyday world by dreaming up a colorful and imaginative place. The moment she walks across this old stone bridge, Alice is in a strange new land filled with all her favorite story-book characters. Help Alice to create the objects, places, and animals of her extraordinary fantasy land—and add your own creative spin to them, too!

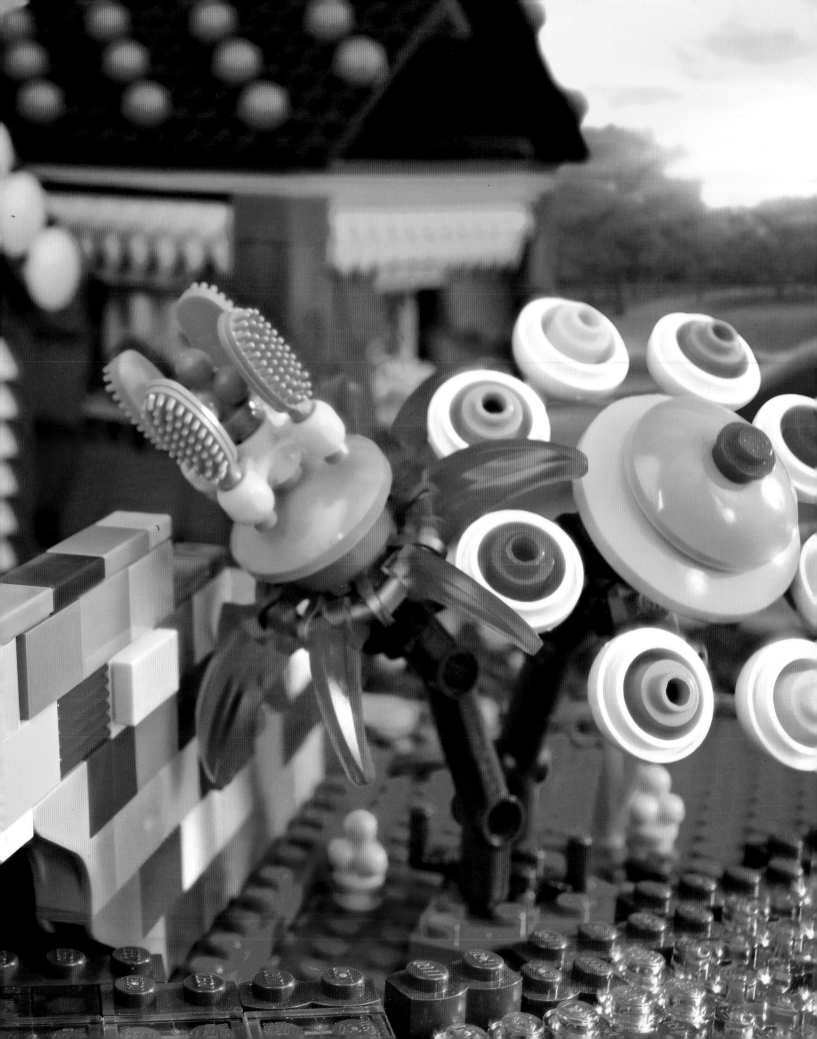

# A fantasy house

None of the colors in this curious little cube-shaped house quite seem to match up! Fantasy buildings are fun to build, even when you don't have lots of pieces with the same colors. You can use whatever colors you like when you're imagining it yourself.

**START HERE**

If you don't have a big plate, make one out of several smaller ones

The first row of plates is indented one stud from the edge

The rows end two studs from the open edge

## 1  Base plate

Start with a big, square base plate. Place a row of two-stud-wide plates near the edges of three sides, and then a one-stud-wide row of plates on top of that.

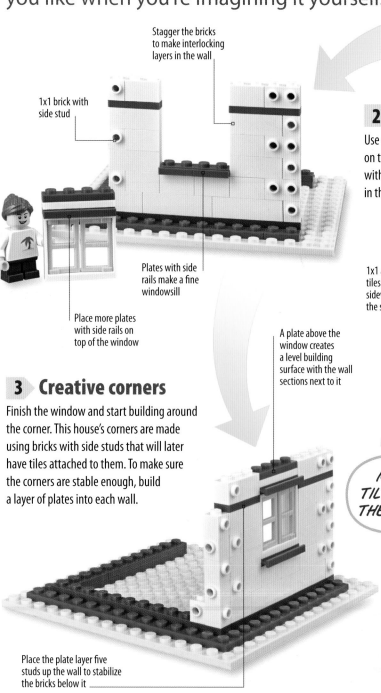

Stagger the bricks to make interlocking layers in the wall

1x1 brick with side stud

Plates with side rails make a fine windowsill

Place more plates with side rails on top of the window

## 2  Think sideways

Use one-stud-wide bricks to start building a wall on top of the tallest plate layer. Position bricks with sideways-facing studs on the ends as shown in the picture. Leave a gap for a window, too.

If you can, make each window's colors different from the other two

1x1 and 1x2 tiles attach sideways to the studs

A plate above the window creates a level building surface with the wall sections next to it

## 3  Creative corners

Finish the window and start building around the corner. This house's corners are made using bricks with side studs that will later have tiles attached to them. To make sure the corners are stable enough, build a layer of plates into each wall.

Place the plate layer five studs up the wall to stabilize the bricks below it

*MORE TILES FOR THE SIDES.*

## 4  Three walls

Build until you have constructed three matching walls, each the same width and with a window in the middle. Keep the center wall one brick-level higher than the two side-walls...for now! Next, attach brightly colored tiles to the side studs on the walls to make decorative brickwork.

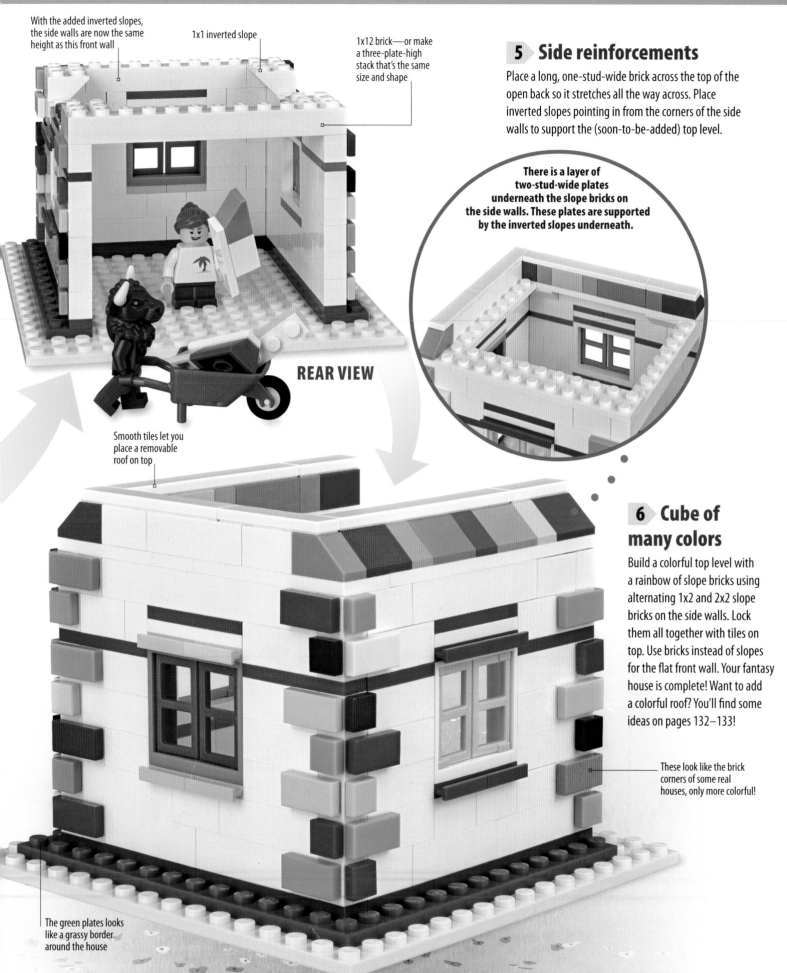

With the added inverted slopes, the side walls are now the same height as this front wall

1x1 inverted slope

1x12 brick—or make a three-plate-high stack that's the same size and shape

## 5 ▶ Side reinforcements

Place a long, one-stud-wide brick across the top of the open back so it stretches all the way across. Place inverted slopes pointing in from the corners of the side walls to support the (soon-to-be-added) top level.

**There is a layer of two-stud-wide plates underneath the slope bricks on the side walls. These plates are supported by the inverted slopes underneath.**

REAR VIEW

Smooth tiles let you place a removable roof on top

## 6 ▶ Cube of many colors

Build a colorful top level with a rainbow of slope bricks using alternating 1x2 and 2x2 slope bricks on the side walls. Lock them all together with tiles on top. Use bricks instead of slopes for the flat front wall. Your fantasy house is complete! Want to add a colorful roof? You'll find some ideas on pages 132–133!

These look like the brick corners of some real houses, only more colorful!

The green plates looks like a grassy border around the house

# Cube village

Arranged around the cube house is a weird and wonderful village of similarly shaped homes, each one different from all of its neighbors. Use your bricks to make these colorful fantasy buildings, or custom-create your own new versions.

**WHAT'S NEXT?**

You've assembled one fantasy-land house. Now you can build more, in lots of varied and multicolored styles.

### Window canopy

This canopy is supported by two 1x2 inverted slopes in the wall. A 1x6 arch on top is locked into the wall by a 2x6 plate, with slopes forming an awning overhead.

**MISMATCH HOUSE**

**A white 2x6 plate in the wall forms a base for six small half arches with matching 1x2 tiles to make this colorful striped awning.**

A line of tiles tops the walls

*THE NEIGHBORS' NEW PAINT JOB IS DELIGHTFUL.*

Stripe is a 2x10 plate inside the wall

Window shutters attached to bricks with clips

### Mismatch house

This detailed little house is surrounded by flowers of multiple sizes. Each of its walls and windows is built in a different way, so you can see something new when you look at it from any angle.

Decorative pattern made from 1x2 textured bricks facing forward and backward

Flowers are stacks of 1x1 round plates, with flower plates at the bases

1x2 plates with handled bars alternate with 1x1 plates with side rings

## Wall panels

The back of each panel on the house is made from regular bricks and bricks with side studs. A plate covered with slopes then attaches to the sideways studs.

The panel fits into this gap in the building frame

Walls are two studs thick to make room for inset sections

There are colorful windowsills inside the building

Upper level built with 1x1 and 2x2 slopes

## COLOR HOUSE

## Color house

From the front, this looks like a classic timber-framed wooden house. But its sides reveal an explosion of color, thanks to a rainbow of slopes built into the walls and roof.

The wall panels on this side feature colorful 1x1 slopes

On this side, the 1x1 slopes are all the same tan color

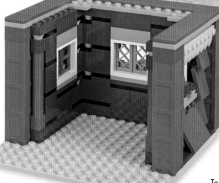

## Scale house

With its scale-like shingled walls and rows of fang-like points, this house looks like a very civilized dragon might live here! Its corners are stacks of 2x2 crates, and flower boxes perch on its windowsills.

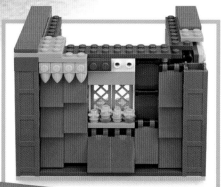

## Shingle walls

Flag-like tiles attach to 1x2 plates with bars built into the wall, with two bricks between each bar-plate level.

REAR VIEW

Tooth plates attached using sideways building

## SCALE HOUSE

Walls are three studs deep to make room for the angled shingles

The bottom row of shingles sticks out more than the rest

# Fantasy roofs gallery

Expand your fantasy world by using a variety of pieces to make colorful and creative rooftops that can be switched from building to building.

The two halves of this roof fit together using 1x2 plates with clips on one side and 1x2 plates with bars on the other.

**BOBBLE-BALL ROOF**

**SLOPED ROOF**

**RICKETY ROOF**

**DORMER ROOF**

YOU'RE QUICK AT BUILDING THESE.

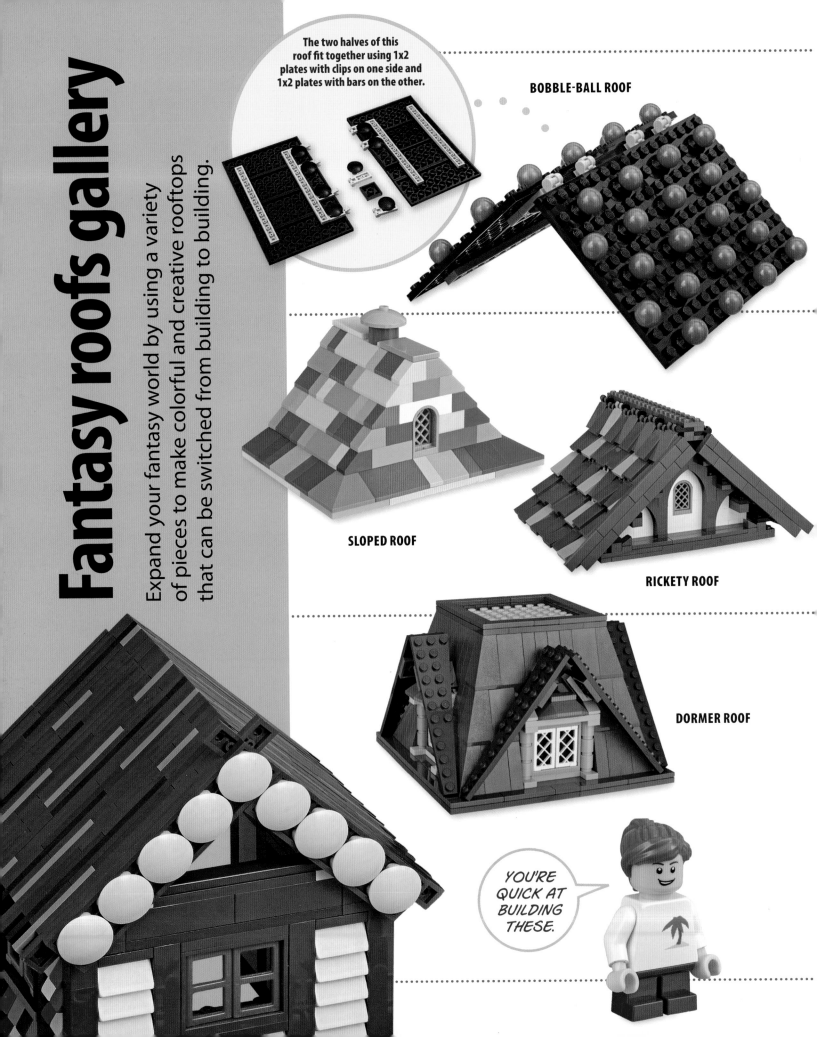

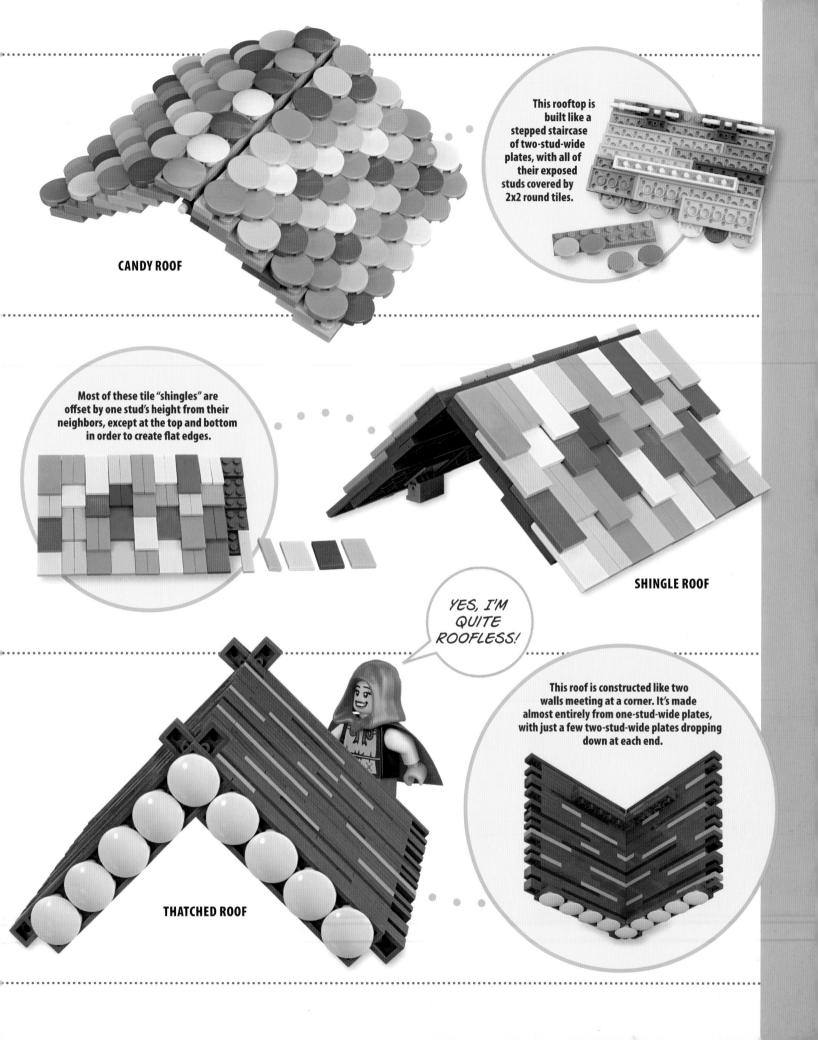

**CANDY ROOF**

This rooftop is built like a stepped staircase of two-stud-wide plates, with all of their exposed studs covered by 2x2 round tiles.

Most of these tile "shingles" are offset by one stud's height from their neighbors, except at the top and bottom in order to create flat edges.

**SHINGLE ROOF**

YES, I'M QUITE ROOFLESS!

This roof is constructed like two walls meeting at a corner. It's made almost entirely from one-stud-wide plates, with just a few two-stud-wide plates dropping down at each end.

**THATCHED ROOF**

# Fences and pathways

Alice departs the village of cube houses and her fantasy land stretches out before her. What path will she take and where will it lead her? She has lots of choices…and so do you!

These flowers are made from triple-scoop ice-cream pieces!

**Build bricks with sideways-facing studs into the edges of your path to let you line it with flowers and plants.**

## Dirt track

This well-worn path is composed of many types of dirt. To make it, build a curvy wall out of bumpy log bricks, and then lay it down on its side.

## Flower fence

Make a fence or wall look more inviting by building an arrangement of flowers on top. In a fantasy land, flowers can look like almost anything!

These double layers of plates hide and lock down the hinge plates

Staggered rows of 1x2 and 1x4 log bricks form a curved shape

Create random, irregular blocks of color for natural-looking patches of earth

2x2 round tiles for big pathway stones

Build in texture with brick-patterned bricks, textured bricks, log bricks, and tiles attached to bricks with side studs

Stepped plates make the side ramps

## Candy cobblestones

In this land, pebbles and stones have the bright colors of candy buttons. A winding path becomes extra-winding when you build in hinges.

**Hidden hinge plates in the path's corners let it move and shift.**

Follow the pathway's shape with curved and angled plates

## Picket fence

This line of fencing uses hinge plates to let it twist and flex. It can go in a straight line, wrap around a building, or create a curvy border to separate one space from another.

Green blades work for big grasses or miniature trees

Switch up hinge plates in front and back for a sinuous curve

## Link fence

Each "link" in this simple but attractive fence is made with just three pieces. Since it only has one-stud connections, you can curve it into almost any shape.

Every link holds its two neighbors together

The links on the ends are at the bottom for balance

**Single and stacked headlight bricks make good fence posts.**

A row of bricks with wheel arches resembles an arching garden fence

**This tiny tree's 1x1 slope branches attach to a 1x1 brick with four studs at its core.**

Green 1x1 cone for the point

Brown 1x1 cone for the trunk

I THINK I PREFER YOUR SIDE.

REALLY? I LONG FOR MUTED TONES.

Tiles cover exposed studs

## Bridge

This bridge separates the real world from the land of fantasy. It has realistic colors and textures at one end, and fantastical ones at the other!

Arched elements for support

# A waterfall

Building a long river could seem like a lengthy task, but you can build up a whole river by making it one smaller section at a time. This plunging waterfall is a model on its own, but it also forms the first part of a flowing fantasy river, which you'll find if you turn the page!

**START HERE**

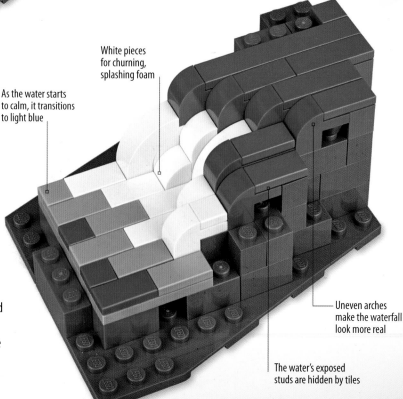

Put the flat sides of two angled plates together for a diagonal base

## 1 ▶ River base

Make a flat base for your river model to rise up from, using angled plates for natural-looking curves and bends. Place a few similar bases end to end, and you've got the start of a river.

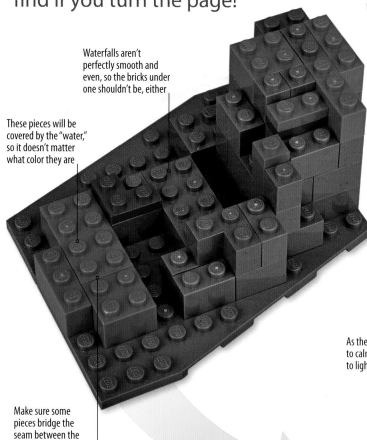

Waterfalls aren't perfectly smooth and even, so the bricks under one shouldn't be, either

These pieces will be covered by the "water," so it doesn't matter what color they are

Make sure some pieces bridge the seam between the two angled plates, to lock them together

## 2 ▶ Rocky rise

Use bricks and plates to build up the river bottom, locking the base plates together. Since this river begins with a waterfall, create a tall brick structure at one end.

White pieces for churning, splashing foam

As the water starts to calm, it transitions to light blue

Uneven arches make the waterfall look more real

The water's exposed studs are hidden by tiles

## 3 ▶ Falling water

The waterfall's plunging water is made using curved half-arch elements built up like steps. Use blue for the slow-moving water at the top, and white where it starts falling fast and getting all churned up.

## 4 ▶ Riverbank

Use gray slopes and bricks to form the waterfall's rocky sides, and log bricks for a packed dirt riverbank. Leave the studs at the top of these bricks exposed so they appear extra rocky and uneven.

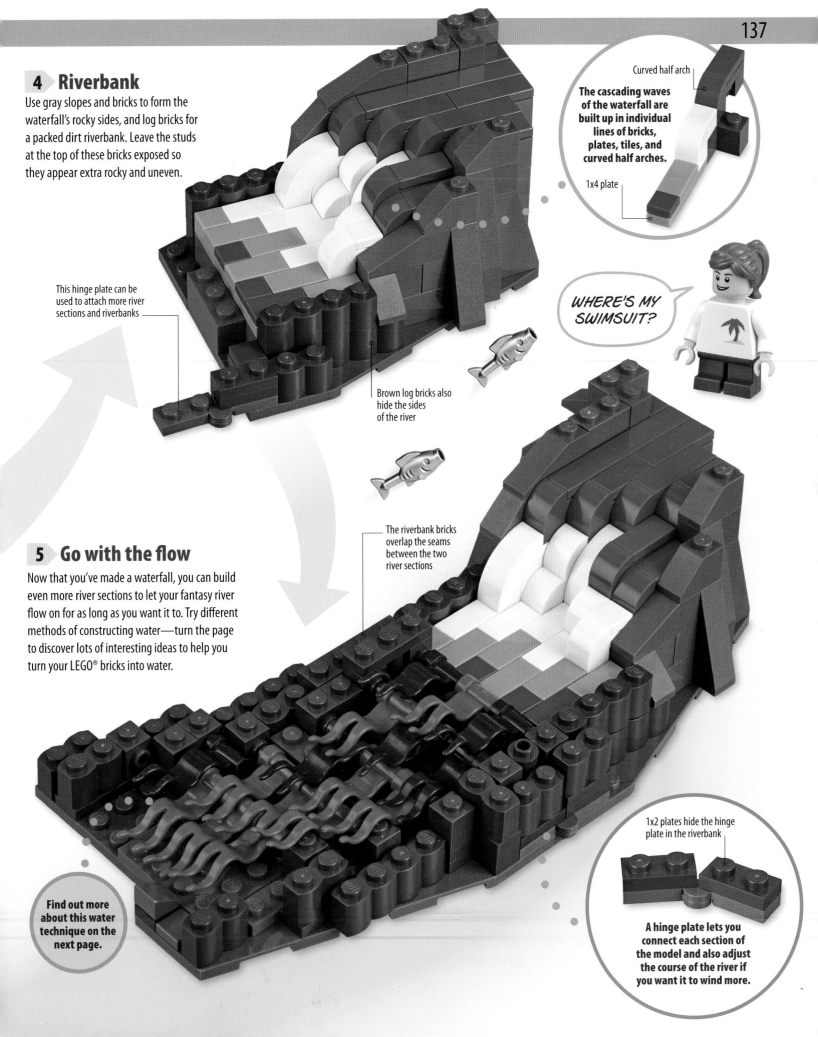

Curved half arch

**The cascading waves of the waterfall are built up in individual lines of bricks, plates, tiles, and curved half arches.**

1x4 plate

This hinge plate can be used to attach more river sections and riverbanks

WHERE'S MY SWIMSUIT?

Brown log bricks also hide the sides of the river

The riverbank bricks overlap the seams between the two river sections

## 5 ▶ Go with the flow

Now that you've made a waterfall, you can build even more river sections to let your fantasy river flow on for as long as you want it to. Try different methods of constructing water—turn the page to discover lots of interesting ideas to help you turn your LEGO® bricks into water.

**Find out more about this water technique on the next page.**

1x2 plates hide the hinge plate in the riverbank

**A hinge plate lets you connect each section of the model and also adjust the course of the river if you want it to wind more.**

# Fantasy river

There are many different ways to build water using your LEGO bricks, and in a fantasy land, one river can feature as many different water effects as you like—this ever-changing river features a few. Can you think of any more?

## WHAT'S NEXT

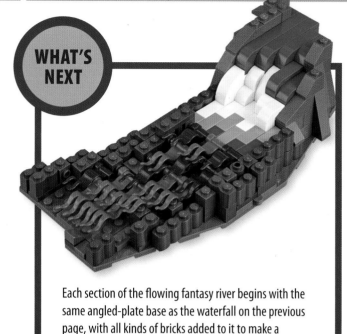

Each section of the flowing fantasy river begins with the same angled-plate base as the waterfall on the previous page, with all kinds of bricks added to it to make a variety of water textures.

## Go with the flow

This magical river changes from tranquil streams to raging rapids at every twist and turn. At each point where the river's building style changes, one hinge plate connects one section to the next.

*I WON'T GET IN. IT'LL RUIN MY MAKEUP.*

Curved slopes make choppy-looking waters

Rows of 1x1 slopes create short, sharp ripples in the water

## Water wall

Make water look as still and clear as glass by building a wall of transparent blue bricks and then laying it down sideways in a matching-shaped space between the riverbank walls.

The streamers all point in the same direction

For fast-running water currents, slide blue streamer pieces onto poles or bars and plug them into riverbank bricks with hollow side studs.

'TIS THE BEST WAY TO KEEP ME CLOTHES CLEAN AND GREEN!

WHO DARES TO BATHE IN MY RIVER?

Use darker blue pieces for the deepest part of the river, and lighter blue for the shallow sides

The water gets bubbly here thanks to the studs on top of 2x2 and 1x1 transparent round plates

### Smooth slope
To depict water flowing gently down a slope, you can layer smooth, transparent blue plates with clips over blue bricks. Create a sloped shape by adding one or two plates underneath the blue bricks.

Lowering the brick by a plate's height leaves space for the clip

# Flower gallery

Flowers here, flowers there...this forest is full of mirthful and magical flowers! Build your own whimsical fantasy flowers by combining unusual LEGO pieces in even more unusual ways.

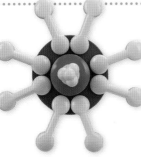

**PHONE FLOWER**

**BOWL FLOWER**

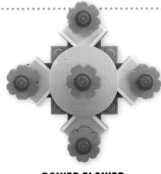

**POWER FLOWER**

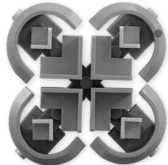

**CORNER FLOWER**

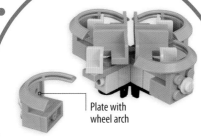

Plate with wheel arch

**The rounded petals of this corner flower are made with 2x2 plates with wheel arches attached sideways.**

**RING FLOWER**

**FLOWER PAD**

**FLOWER STEMS**

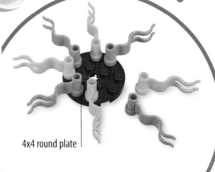

4x4 round plate

**The streamer petals are attached to the studs around the edge of a plate at this flower's base.**

**SUNBURST FLOWER**

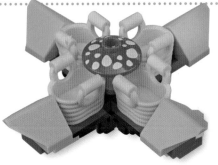

**FORAGING FLOWER**

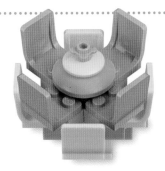

**CHAIR FLOWER**

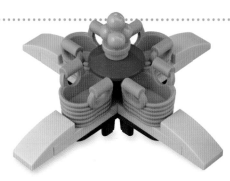

**BOBBLE BASKET FLOWER**

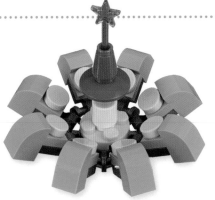

**MAGIC FLOWER**

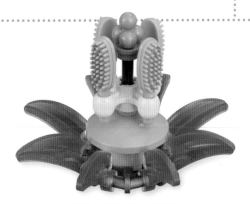

**HAIRBRUSH FLOWER**

**VINE FLOWER**

**FLOWER PATCHES**

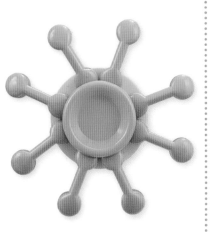

**DISH FLOWER**

**BOWL REED**

**SNAKE REED**

**SURFBOARD REED**

# Fantasy creatures

As she walks through her fantasy forest, Alice encounters everything from giant butterflies to tiny, trilling dragons. What other marvelous and mystical creatures might you spy in your own fantasy forest?

## Giant butterfly

Alice can hardly believe her eyes at this butterfly's size! It's big in real-brick scale, but compared to a minifigure, it's positively enormous. Use arches and slopes to give the wings their shapes, and bricks and plates to create one-of-a-kind wing patterns.

Antennae elements for antennae!

Make your butterflies whatever colors you want—the more vivid, the better!

A 1x2 plate locks the inverted curved slopes together

A half arch piece makes a scalloped edge

Bricks with vertical bars on the wings snap into pairs of clips built into the body

## Butterfly body

Most of the butterfly's body is a stack of 1x2 plates and bricks, with 1x1 plates with clips to connect the handles on the wings. Small brackets at the front and back provide studs for attaching curved slopes on top.

**Build bricks with round holes into the wings, then plug in the studs of 1x1 round bricks to make colorful 3-D details.**

A clip-and-bar hinge attaches the pointed wing extension

# Mini dragons

Build tiny dragons to inhabit your fantasy forest using small pieces with complementary colors. Attach the wings to clips so they can flap up and down.

1x1 slopes for angled snouts and armored spikes

Dragon wing piece attaches to a 1x1 plate with top clip

ROAAAR!

Add tooth plates for legs

Tooth plate on back can face in either direction

BIT GRUMPY, AREN'T WE?

Transparent 1x1 round plate makes a glowing eye

## Dragon details

The whole dragon is constructed around a 1x1 brick with studs on its top and all four sides. Elements with clips, bars, and detail-shapes are built out from it in all directions but down.

Base of head is a 1x2 plate with bar

1x1 brick with four side studs

Slope tail attaches to a small bracket

WHERE ARE ALL THE PLANTS?

This caterpillar's body segments are made from either two ball or two socket joints, which are held together by sliding plates underneath and sideways-facing brackets on top.

## Giant caterpillars

Big, round eyes make these many-legged insects look more cute than creepy. Build a series of identical segments and attach them in a jointed chain to create their flexible bodies.

Joysticks for movable bug antennae

Printed round 1x1 tile eyes, attached to an angle-plate bracket with two side studs

These body sections are made from tow-ball and hitch plates, giving the assembled model a great side-to-side wiggling, scuttling movement.

Antennae made from minifigure handcuffs

Legs made from 1x2 three-tooth plates

BEATS ME.

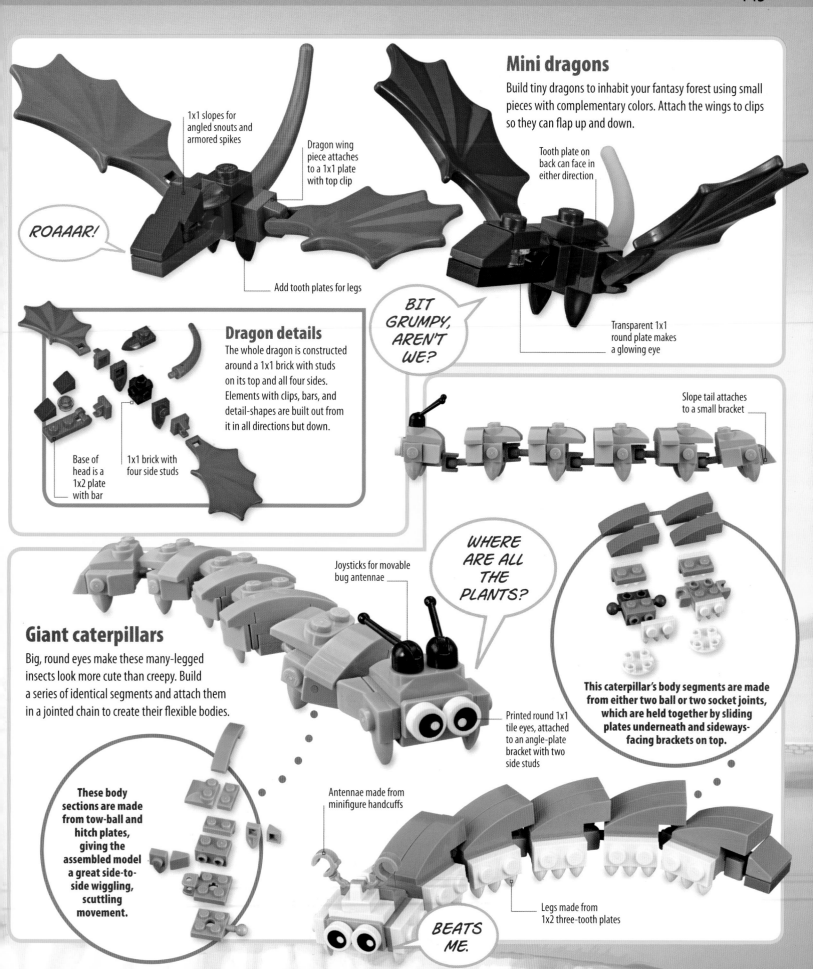

# Tree slide

Imagine the fun things you can add to the trees of a fantasy forest. How about a fairy's home or a dragon's nest? Or a magical slide that takes you on a speedy, twisting trip down the tallest tree in the woods?

## Crow's nest

At the top of the slide is a platform with railings, so you can look out and see the entire forest all around. It's built with three 4x4 quarter-circle plates and extra rectangular plates to make the spacing fit perfectly with the start of the slide.

Leaves can be spread out around the tree, or clustered in dense bunches

Mix different leaf colors for realistic shades

Safety railings made from curved and straight fence pieces

1x2 tiles lock the railings together

The top of the slide sits level with the platform

1x1 cone for the tapered end of a branch

## Building branches

Angled LEGO Technic connectors, held together by short cross axles, let you build the branches so that they grow in every direction, like those of a real tree. The leaf pieces are held on by bars, pushed into the tops of LEGO Technic pins with hollow studs.

LEGO® Technic pin connects the bar to the connector hole

Bricks with holes connect the branches to the trunk

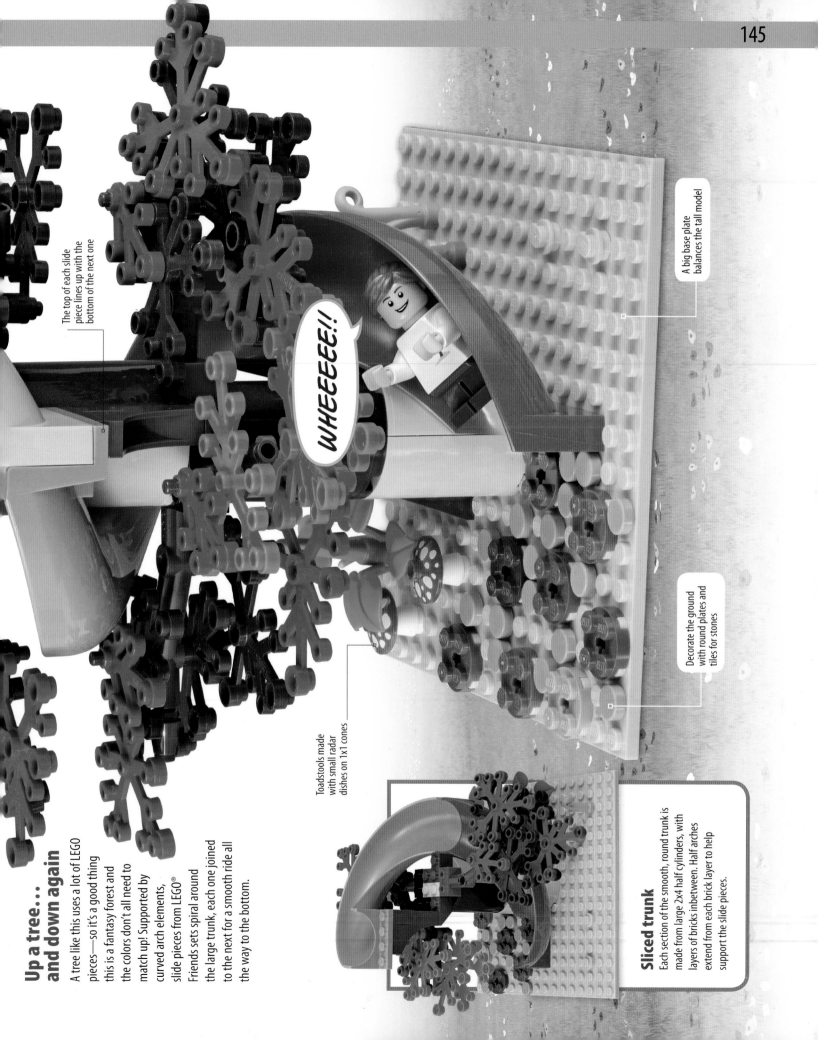

# Up a tree... and down again

A tree like this uses a lot of LEGO pieces—so it's a good thing this is a fantasy forest and the colors don't all need to match up! Supported by curved arch elements, slide pieces from LEGO® Friends sets spiral around the large trunk, each one joined to the next for a smooth ride all the way to the bottom.

The top of each slide piece lines up with the bottom of the next one

A big base plate balances the tall model

Decorate the ground with round plates and tiles for stones

Toadstools made with small radar dishes on 1x1 cones

WHEEEEEE!!

## Sliced trunk

Each section of the smooth, round trunk is made from large 2x4 half cylinders, with layers of bricks inbetween. Half arches extend from each brick layer to help support the slide pieces.

Use two curved railing pieces for a half-circle or one for a quarter-circle

Doorway leads to a slide

JUST MONKEYING AROUND.

# Tree-house

In a very large tree in Alice's fantasy forest is a magnificent tree-house. It has been built right into the middle of the tree, with its door at the base and rooms that go all the way up its trunk.

## Home in the woods

Use brown bricks and curved arches to build a sturdy trunk for your tree-house. Support the floors of the hollow spaces from underneath, and secure your pieces together with lots of interlocking plates so that they won't fall apart. Include some decorative touches like furnishings, terraces with railings, and a stairway lined with flowerpots.

## Living room

At the bottom of the trunk is a cozy furnished room with a couch, bookshelf, drawers, and a sink. The patterned floor mixes smooth tiles with 2x2 jumper plates that have studs where minifigures can stand.

## The modular tree

Each of the tree's three sections is built separately. Their tops are lined with tiles with just a couple of studs, so that they can be taken apart and played with or moved around.

The brick walls of the trunk are staggered to make it stable

Branches made from LEGO Technic connectors, 1x1 cones, and leaf elements connected by pins and bars

Each flowerpot attaches to a 1x2 jumper plate on top of a 1x2 brick

Small staircase made of 1x4 plates with one stud at each end leads up to the balcony

Staggered inverted arches create realistic root shapes

A stone path made from round plates and tiles leads to the front door

**EXPLODED VIEW**

# A castle wall

Bonk! What could Alice have just walked into? Why, it's the wall of a grand castle! Start your own fantasy castle by building a rainbow-colored wall, with connectors on the sides so that it can attach to other walls with the same design.

**START HERE**

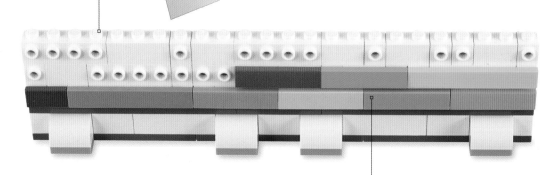

The plates lock the bricks above and below them together

Curved slopes make smooth and stud-free feet

## 1 > Fantastic foundation

How do you build a strong standing wall? Begin with a solid, two-stud-wide foundation base made of bricks... and add feet so it won't fall over! Plate layers provide attractive stripes.

You can use 1x1, 1x2, or 1x4 bricks with side studs

## 2 > Studs and tiles

Build up the wall with one-stud-wide bricks. Include bricks with studs on their sides, all pointing in the same direction, so that you can decorate the front and leave the back plain. Snap colored tiles onto the studs in a staggered pattern.

Make sure each tile is attached to at least two studs so it won't fall off

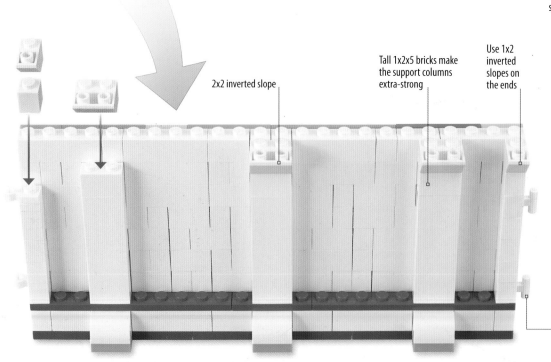

2x2 inverted slope

Tall 1x2x5 bricks make the support columns extra-strong

Use 1x2 inverted slopes on the ends

## 3 > Supports and modular connectors

At the back of the wall, stack up 1x2 bricks into columns above each rear-facing foot, topping them with inverted slopes. Build similar 1x1 stacks at each edge, incorporating plates with clips on one end and bricks with handled bars on the other.

Line up the clips and handles so they would snap together if you had two matching walls next to each other

## 4 ▶ Wall-top walkway

Snap down a layer of plates to lock the bricks at the top of the wall together with the support columns' inverted slopes. On top of this layer, attach a line of four-stud-wide plates to create a wide walkway.

An additional line of one-stud-wide plates make a wider, flat base for the walkway

The walkway sticks out over the edge of the wall by one stud's width

THESE DEFENSES BETTER BE SECURE, BUILDER!

You could cover the walkway with tiles, but studs will let you attach minifigures

For a more realistic stone wall, substitute gray tiles for the rainbow-hued ones shown here. Use a variety of gray shades as different types of stones.

The studs on the parapet resemble the stone blocks of real castle battlements

## 5 ▶ Parapet

As a final touch, add a short parapet wall of one-stud-wide bricks along the front edge of the walkway. Now the castle's guards won't fall over the edge—and they have something to duck down behind if enemies attack!

# More castle walls

With the clips and handles on the sides of your wall, you can build multiple segments and snap them together to form a castle circumference of any size. Make your walls match, or mix things up with these fanciful designs.

**WHAT'S NEXT?**

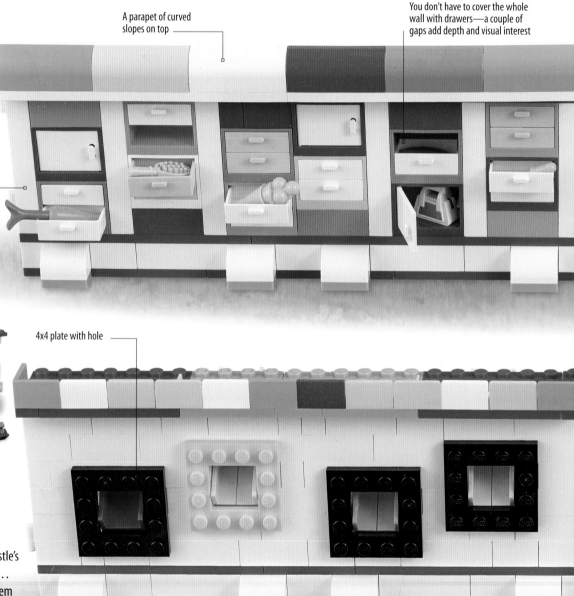

Each of these walls starts on the same foundation as the one on the previous pages. The difference lies in how you build it up from there!

A parapet of curved slopes on top

You don't have to cover the whole wall with drawers—a couple of gaps add depth and visual interest

## Cupboard wall

You've probably heard of a chest of drawers, but how about an entire wall of them? This wall alternates one-stud-wide brick columns with opening LEGO drawer and cabinet elements. It's the perfect place to stow your treasures or your spare carrots!

Use tall column bricks or stacks of shorter ones

Double-thickness sections reinforce the wall

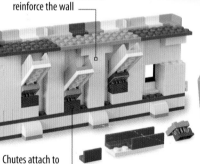

4x4 plate with hole

Chutes attach to two-part hinges

**REAR VIEW**

## Chute wall

The slide-like chutes on this wall let your castle's defenders roll stones onto hostile attackers… or send food down to beloved pets. Build them with small wall panels on plates, held at an angle by a snap-together hinge.

## Arch wall

The white bricks of this wall are built one row of studs back on the foundation base, making room for a lattice-like pattern of curved half-arch elements. The parapet rail on top is made from smaller half arches with a similar curved shape.

Make all of your arches the same color, or combine different colors

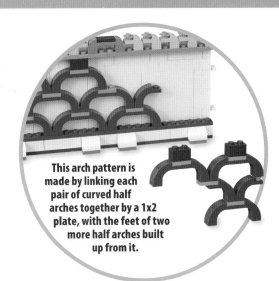

**This arch pattern is made by linking each pair of curved half arches together by a 1x2 plate, with the feet of two more half arches built up from it.**

1x1 flower plate decoration

Use 1x1 round or square plates to connect arches at the wall's edge

Curved half arches locked together by 1x2 tile form defensive battlements

**Each "bump" on this woven wall is made from curved slope bricks locked together with a plate underneath.**

Use curved slopes of different lengths to make longer or shorter "bumps"

## Woven wall

This wall uses curved slopes to make rounded stripe shapes. They're attached to sideways-built plates and staggered to resemble the texture of a woven straw basket.

# Castle walls (continued)

**Build the color bricks into a second wall behind the first one—make sure you lock both walls together securely!**

White bricks fill the spaces between window frames

## Window-frame wall

Empty white window frames of different shapes and sizes, with blocks of colored bricks behind them, make this wall look like the artwork of painter Piet Mondrian. A smooth walkway with a latticed parapet enhances its classic-yet-colorful style.

Frames can be squares or long or tall rectangles

Connect long tiles to inverted 1x2 brackets for the parapet wall

**Create a staggered tile design by lining up bricks with side studs in even rows, then attaching the tiles at either their top or bottom.**

## Tiled wall

Make a tiled pattern by attaching 2x2 square tiles onto rows of bricks with side studs built into your wall. For extra texture and variety, sprinkle in a bunch of 2x2 jumper plates with central studs, too.

Wall indented by one stud

WHAT'S THE PASSWORD?

Railing made from tiles attached to 1x1 bricks with side studs

To connect the baskets, build a plate layer into the wall and leave some one-stud-wide gaps for the basket hole to fit onto.

PASS!

If you don't have baskets, try attaching small wall panels and corner panels on top of an inverted slope to make a box with sides

## Flowerpot wall

Here's a new idea: a castle wall decorated with flowerpots! Space the baskets apart so that there is room to place small accessories inside. Fill them with flowers, or put something different into each one.

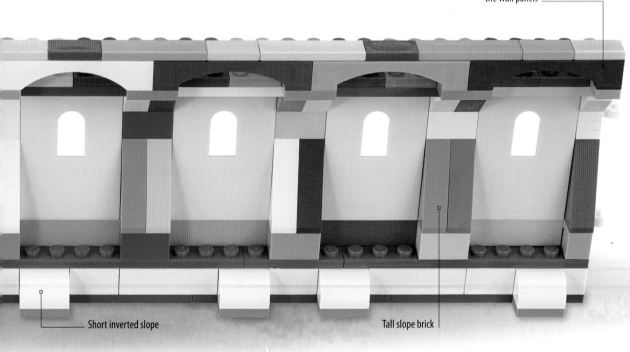

Arches go over the wall panels

## Paneled wall

This wall design makes use of LEGO castle wall panels with cut-out windows, and places slope elements between them for structural bracing. Bigger at the bottom and smaller at the top, the braces add stability and support the top walkway.

Short inverted slope

Tall slope brick

# A castle tower

The next step in building your fantasy castle is constructing a tower, like the ones that Alice can see rising high overhead. Use big wall panels arranged in a circle for its cylinder shape, and angled plates and hinges to construct a cone-shaped top.

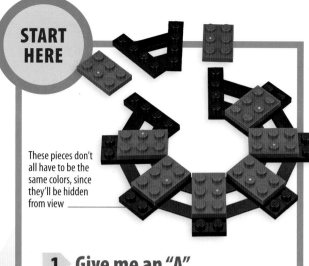

START HERE

These pieces don't all have to be the same colors, since they'll be hidden from view

## 1 ▶ Give me an "A"

The key element for making this build is the A-shaped plate piece. Start with eight of them, laid edge-to-edge to form a wheel-like ring. Then use eight 2x3 plates to connect them all together and create a stable base for your tower.

## 2 ▶ Walls and round bits

Place a castle wall panel onto each "spoke" of the wheel—eight in total. Attach a 1x1 flower plate under the bottom corner of each panel so there aren't any big gaps underneath, and a 1x1 round brick on each upper corner.

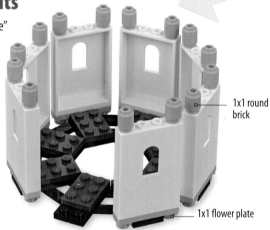

1x1 round brick

1x1 flower plate

## 4 ▶ Roof cone

To build the conical tower top, start with eight left-facing and eight right-facing 3x8 triangular plates (these plates are mirror images of each other). Connect one of each type together with 2x4 plates underneath to make four 6x8 wedges. Use snap-together hinges to place them above every second wall panel. Fill in the four empty spaces with 4x9 wedge plates on the same type of hinges.

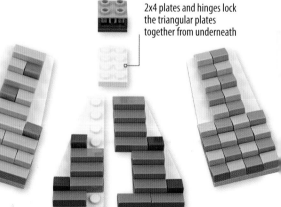

2x4 plates and hinges lock the triangular plates together from underneath

## 3 ▶ Tower sandwich

Secure the walls together solidly by laying down a second ring of eight A-shaped plates on top of the assembly, creating a wall-panel sandwich. Use eight 2x4 plates to lock them together. Your tower base should be good and strong now.

**5** **A tower is born!**

Swing the roof wedges inwards to form a cone, and your castle tower is done! To make it taller, you could build a stack of additional tower sections below this one. Now you can add floors and furnishings inside, or place decorative details on the outside for all in your fantasy kingdom to see.

THIS IS THE PERFECT SPOT FOR MY NEST.

Decorate the studded surfaces of the roof—1x1 slopes make great roof shingles

A patchwork of slope colors suits a fantasy castle well

The longer wedges hang down one stud lower than the short wedges

Don't have 16 A-shaped plates? You can build similar tower designs using angled plates or bent hinge plates.

# Fancy towers

More towers rise from the castle, in a myriad of designs. Try round towers, square towers, towers with windows, arches, and doors— even towers made of boats. Include clips and handles to connect them to your castle walls.

**WHAT'S NEXT?**

You've already seen one way to build one type of tower for your castle. Now look at these other imaginative methods.

**ROWBOAT**

**HEXAGON**

## Rowboat tower

LEGO boats filled with decorative brick mosaics provide this stately tower with its Gothic-style peaked arches. Other details include ornate columns with round-brick corners, and a conical spire.

Two large half-cones topped with a 4x4 and 2x2 cone

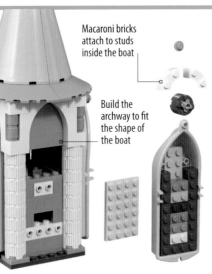

Macaroni bricks attach to studs inside the boat

Build the archway to fit the shape of the boat

## Archways

The underside of the boat is pressed onto a 4x6 plate. The plate is then attached sideways to bricks with side studs built into the recessed archways in the tower walls.

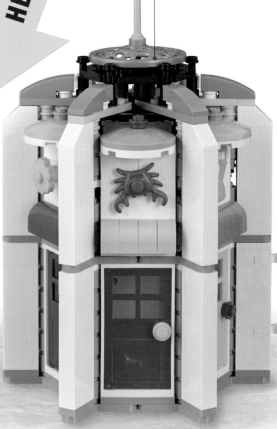

If you don't have this filigreed golden wheel, you could use a radar dish piece

## Hexagon tower

This tower is built on a base of propeller-like, three-ended plates. Each of its eight sides bears a door, a curved awning, and a decorative ornament above.

## MACARONI

## FAIRY-TALE

## FORTRESS

Round railing made from curved fence pieces

## Macaroni tower

Combine large macaroni bricks in multiple colors to build a round tower with spiraling stripes like a lighthouse. A stack of bricks inside reinforces the hollow structure to make it strong.

Light blue half arches make a pointed arch

Octagonal plates at the top and bottom

Tall 1x1x5 bricks for sturdy corner columns

## Fairy-tale tower

This storybook-style tower has arched frames around its windows, and an open-walled turret on top. Each side uses the same building techniques, but with different brick variations and color combinations.

Thanks to hinge bricks, this tower could have as many sides as you like

Extended wall fills the gap between sides

Inverted slope bricks support the overhanging tower top

Windowsill made from a row of 1x1 plates with side rings

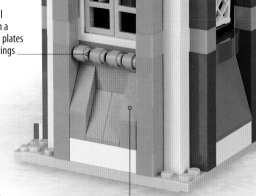

## Fortress tower

Except for its fanciful colors, this six-sided tower could be part of a medieval lord's stone fort. Its edges are linked together by hinge-bricks, and have patterns of white bricks that resemble masonry blocks called "quoin corners."

The angled design is made mostly from slope bricks

# Castle features

What other features besides towers and catapults can you add to your fantasy castle? You could build a grand entrance archway to welcome new visitors to the kingdom…or decorate your castle courtyard with a dazzling ice-cream cone fountain!

While you could build your own arches out of smaller pieces, using a single arch-shaped element will make your model stronger and able to support more weight.

1x2 brick with axle hole

1x1 flower plate on a 1x1 round brick

Grooved pattern made with the fronts and backs of 1x2 textured bricks

Climbing vines are leaf elements attached to bricks with side studs

For a cobbled castle floor, place a variety of round gray and brown plates and tiles on top of gray plates

Slope bricks create a wider and sturdier base for the gatehouse wall

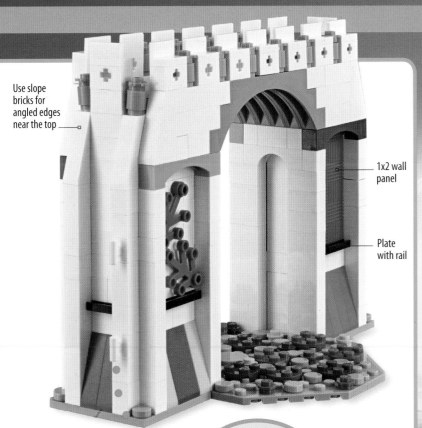

Use slope bricks for angled edges near the top

1x2 wall panel

Plate with rail

**SIDE VIEW**

The bottom of the axle plugs into a 2x2 round brick to connect it to the fountain base

## Ice-cream fountain

The fountain's ice-cream-scoop top is built with four quarter-dome pieces on a 6x6 round plate. It is supported by a stack of two 2x2 round bricks and a plate, which are pushed onto a long LEGO Technic axle and hidden inside a tan-colored drill for a cone.

> Clips and handles on the sides of the gatehouse can connect to the castle wall models and castle towers. Turn to pages 162–164 to see how they all fit together.

## Gatehouse arch

A gatehouse provides a way for friends to pass through the castle's high wall. Build it to be tall and wide so that riders and wagons can go through, too. Add interesting features to enliven its flat sides, and detail the ground underneath with dirt and stones.

This fountain's ice-cream cone shape is no coincidence—on festival days, it sprays ice cream instead of water!

## Fountain

Whether ornately elegant or festive and fun, a fountain can really brighten up a fantasy castle's courtyard and other open spaces. There are hundreds of ways to build one. Start with a wall around a water-filled base, then add a high spout in the middle.

> I WISH EVERY DAY WAS CHOCOLATE FOUNTAIN DAY.

Use blue for water, or add colored pieces inside the fountain wall to represent different ice-cream flavors

4x4 curved plates for a base

Curved wall made with large macaroni bricks

Place catapults on your castle's wall, at the top of a tower, or on the ground nearby.

You can also make the side walls taller to give the throwing arm more movement

HMM, PERHAPS WE SHOULD DELIVER OUR PIES BY BIKE?

Tiles on base add decoration and weight

A 1x2 slope helps to brace the side wall

# Cream-pie catapult

How does a castle in a silly fantasy land defend itself? With a catapult that launches messy cream pies! To build a working LEGO catapult, just combine a sturdy support base with a swinging throwing arm. Here's how to do it!

### 1 Base and pivot plate

Start with a wide, stable base plate. Build two side walls with round holes in their middles. Plug two free-spinning LEGO Technic pins into a 2x2 plate with rings underneath. Snap one of the pins into the hole in each wall, and attach the walls with the plate between them onto the base.

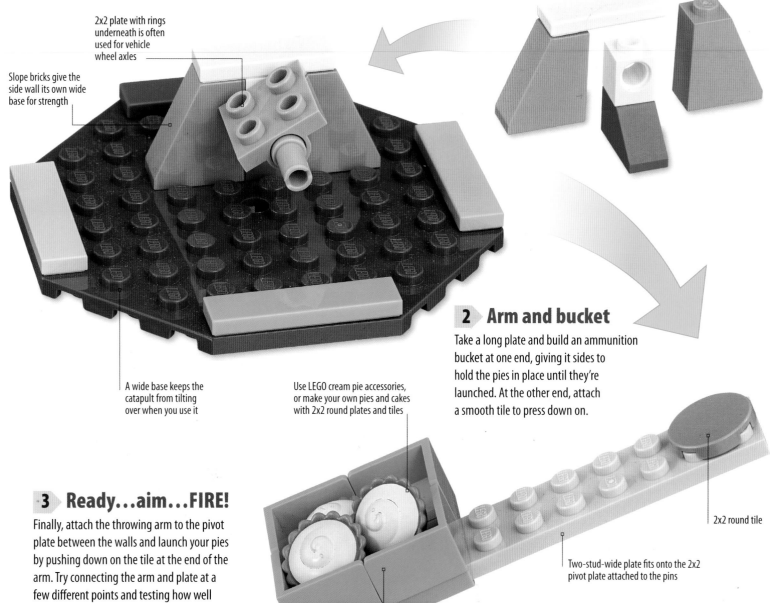

2x2 plate with rings underneath is often used for vehicle wheel axles

Slope bricks give the side wall its own wide base for strength

A wide base keeps the catapult from tilting over when you use it

Use LEGO cream pie accessories, or make your own pies and cakes with 2x2 round plates and tiles

### 2 Arm and bucket

Take a long plate and build an ammunition bucket at one end, giving it sides to hold the pies in place until they're launched. At the other end, attach a smooth tile to press down on.

2x2 round tile

Two-stud-wide plate fits onto the 2x2 pivot plate attached to the pins

Bucket made from four 2x2 corner panels on a 4x4 plate— or use four 1x1 corners and four 1x2 wall panels to make the same shape

### 3 Ready...aim...FIRE!

Finally, attach the throwing arm to the pivot plate between the walls and launch your pies by pushing down on the tile at the end of the arm. Try connecting the arm and plate at a few different points and testing how well your cakes fly. A long throwing arm means a greater pie-tossing distance, but an arm that's too long will be harder to fire. Practice until you find just the right balance!

# The castle complete

Alice stares at the complete castle—a riotous rainbow of colors and shapes, with no two parts the same. She has never seen anything so spectacular! Without wasting another moment, she takes a deep breath and steps through the gateway. What wonders will her imagination find on the other side?

Add flags in different colors for a regal decoration

IT'S PIE-THROWING TIME.

I'LL NEVER GET THIS PIE CREAM OUT OF MY FUR.

I WANT MY MUMMY!

## A modular castle

You've built walls, towers, and a gatehouse. Now put them all together to create your castle! Thanks to the clip-and-bar hinge connections that you've given each of the modular sections, you can position your castle wall in the shape of a circle, a square, or even a multi-pointed star! Put the fountain in the middle, and add catapults or any other castle features that you want to build.

Take the sections apart and rearrange them however you like!

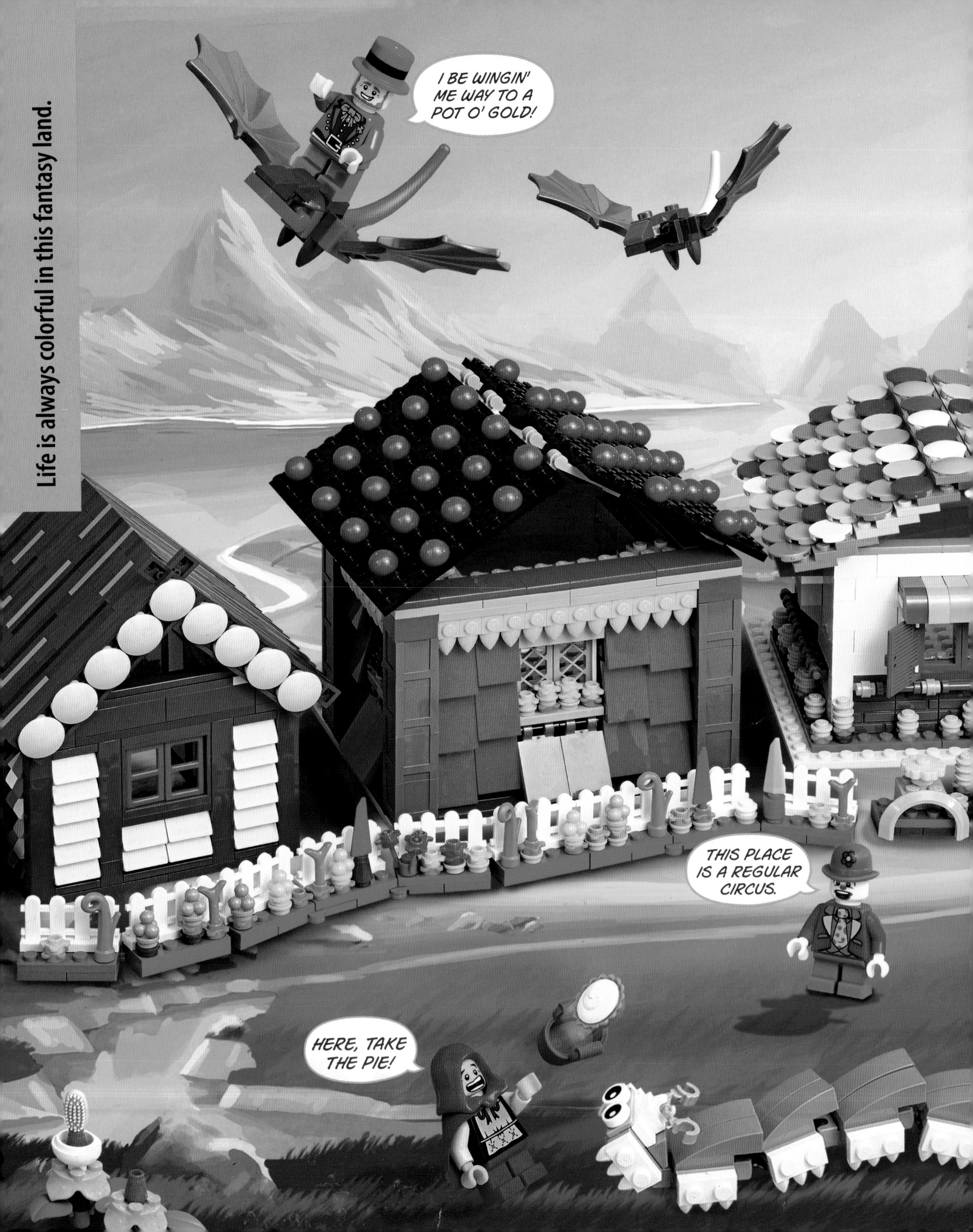

Life is always colorful in this fantasy land.

# THE REAL WORLD

Spaceman Tech 4 from the space colony on the planet Volga (see Chapter 1) was on a routine research excursion when he found himself sucked into an unknown new dimension where everything is HUGE. Before help arrives, Tech 4 plans to piece together some information about the giant artifacts he can see. Explore this strange human world with him—and bring him some extra pieces for building big!

# A cell phone

Is that a massive black monolith, towering over this strange world? No—it's a life-sized cell phone made from LEGO® pieces! Use plates and tiles to build your own realistic model phone for play or display.

**START HERE**

You can also put smaller plates together—just make sure the pieces you place on top lock them together well!

## 1 Brick technology

To build a flat, rectangular device, start with a flat, rectangular building surface. A 6x12 plate makes a perfect base for a sleek, black cellular telephone.

## 2 A thin layer

Keep your phone thin and streamlined by covering its flat areas with smooth tiles. Use single-studded jumper plates as connection points for buttons and other projecting details.

Make an even pattern of studs for even rows of buttons

1x1 round brick plugged into a 2x2 plate with a round hole in its side

A printed 2x2 tile makes a good speaker—or use a pair of 1x2 grilles

A 4x4 square of gray tiles for a screen

POCKET SIZED?

## 3 Add the details

Now attach the pieces that will make this recognizable as a cell phone, such as buttons, a speaker, accept/reject buttons, and (if you want to go a little old-school) an antenna on top.

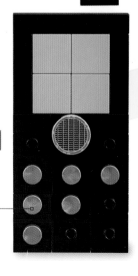

Use 1x1 round or square tiles for buttons

Colored tiles for accept/reject buttons

## 4 Beepity-boop

Your new phone is finished! Just don't accidentally mix it up with the real thing when you leave the house. Plastic bricks aren't good at making long-distance calls!

# Technology

What other pocket-sized tech devices can you build using the same construction techniques as the cell phone? You could put together a calculator… or an MP3 player to store and play all of your favorite imaginary tunes.

**MP3 PLAYER**

Printed or stickered tiles for icons

**WHAT'S NEXT?**

Starting with the same kind of base plate as the cell phone, change around the details to create different devices.

## MP3 player

The key is to make your models look like what they're supposed to be with a few key details. Add screen icons and a round wheel to a music player, and its identity quickly becomes clear!

2x2 round tile attached to a 2x2 plate

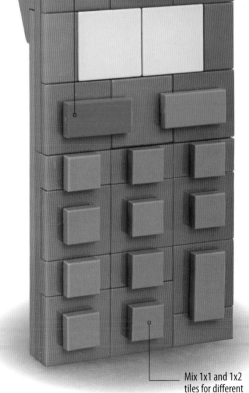

1x2 tiles are attached to 2x2 jumper plates

This 1x3 tile goes across two 2x2 jumper plates

**CALCULATOR**

Mix 1x1 and 1x2 tiles for different button shapes

## Calculator

Try taking a look at the real thing before you build your LEGO brick version. The angled back and button layout make this calculator model seem extra-authentic.

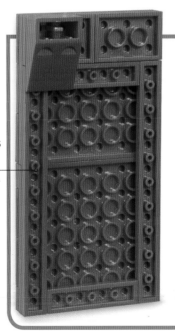

Extra layer of plates holds two 6x6 plates together in a 6x12 shape

Inverted angled bottom

2x3 studded top

## Angled back

A row of inverted slopes on the back makes the calculator rest at an angle when set down.

# Stationery

Behold these bizarre human tools that sit atop a vast and featureless plane. It seems to be a gigantic desk covered with writing and art supplies! Be inspired by everyday items like stationery to make something ordinary look extraordinary.

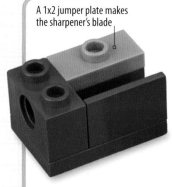

A 1x2 jumper plate makes the sharpener's blade

This eraser is made from just three pieces: a 1x4 brick and two 1x2 tiles

A 1x4 tile on top hides the studs

## Pencil sharpener and eraser

Even a small handful of pieces can let you create stationery tools. Build them next to the real ones so you get the details and proportions right.

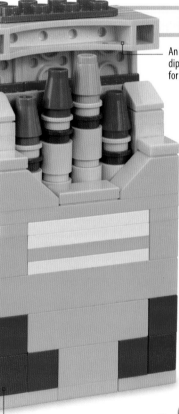

An arch on the lid and a dip on the box make a gap for a finger to flip it open

The lid opens on a row of three 1x2 snap-together hinges

Grilles attached to side studs mimic a bar code on the back

Crayon wrappers are identical stacks of tan and brown 1x1 round bricks and plates

Build colorful pieces into the walls of the box for decoration

## Crayon box

This box has a hinged lid that flips back to store the crayons inside. It can take a bit of practice to build one object that fits inside another, but the end result is worth it!

HMM, I ALWAYS THOUGHT I WAS TALLER.

REAR VIEW

## Ruler

Make a ruler by stacking up plates —white for the main body, and black for the lines. Altogether, this model is four studs across and 62 plates high!

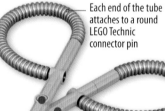

Each end of the tube attaches to a round LEGO Technic connector pin

The two identical scissor halves are attached together by a pivoting, free-spinning LEGO® Technic connector pin.

Decorative swords can be found in LEGO® NINJAGO™ sets

## Scissors

These scissors can't cut, but they can open and close just like the real thing. Use straight LEGO Technic connectors and flexible tubes to make the handles, and LEGO sword pieces for the blades.

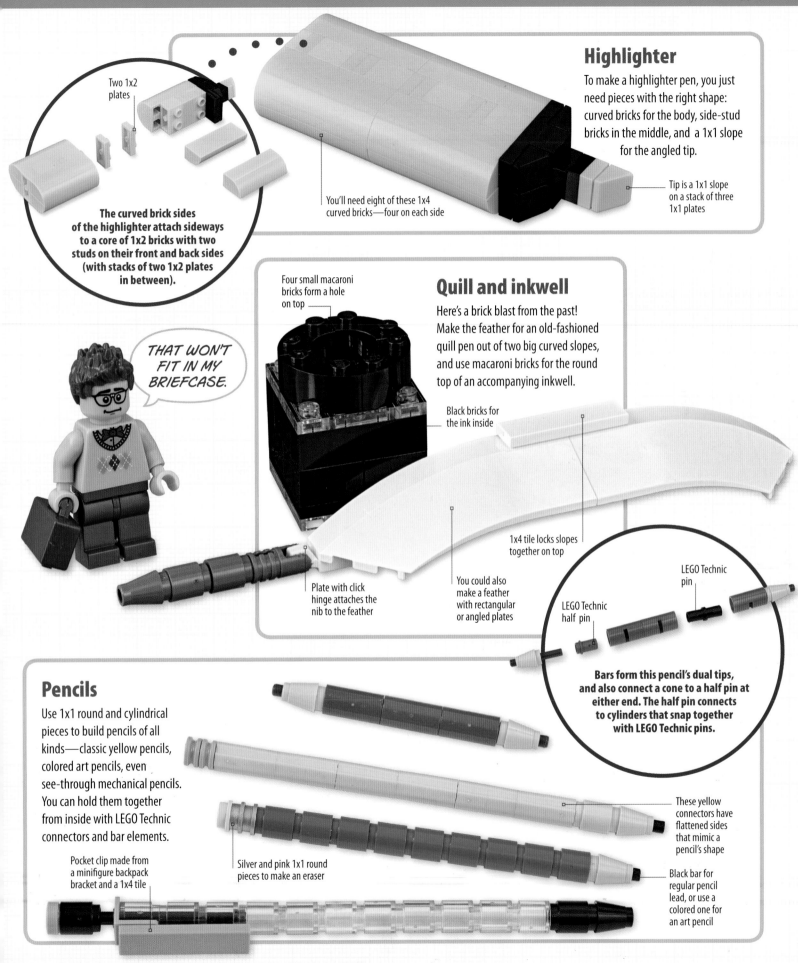

## Highlighter

To make a highlighter pen, you just need pieces with the right shape: curved bricks for the body, side-stud bricks in the middle, and a 1x1 slope for the angled tip.

Two 1x2 plates

The curved brick sides of the highlighter attach sideways to a core of 1x2 bricks with two studs on their front and back sides (with stacks of two 1x2 plates in between).

You'll need eight of these 1x4 curved bricks—four on each side

Tip is a 1x1 slope on a stack of three 1x1 plates

## Quill and inkwell

Here's a brick blast from the past! Make the feather for an old-fashioned quill pen out of two big curved slopes, and use macaroni bricks for the round top of an accompanying inkwell.

Four small macaroni bricks form a hole on top

THAT WON'T FIT IN MY BRIEFCASE.

Black bricks for the ink inside

1x4 tile locks slopes together on top

Plate with click hinge attaches the nib to the feather

You could also make a feather with rectangular or angled plates

LEGO Technic pin

LEGO Technic half pin

Bars form this pencil's dual tips, and also connect a cone to a half pin at either end. The half pin connects to cylinders that snap together with LEGO Technic pins.

## Pencils

Use 1x1 round and cylindrical pieces to build pencils of all kinds—classic yellow pencils, colored art pencils, even see-through mechanical pencils. You can hold them together from inside with LEGO Technic connectors and bar elements.

These yellow connectors have flattened sides that mimic a pencil's shape

Pocket clip made from a minifigure backpack bracket and a 1x4 tile

Silver and pink 1x1 round pieces to make an eraser

Black bar for regular pencil lead, or use a colored one for an art pencil

WOOO HOOO!

I'M USED TO BEING WEIGHTLESS!

2x4 plate with three round holes

The heavier the weight on top, the more the dial moves

**7 Final model**

When the weighing plate's axle is pushed down, it pushes on the catch and pin, moving the dial on the outside of the scale. Let go, and it springs back up!

**6 Pan attachment**

Attach the plate with holes on the weighing pan attachment to the top of the scale, so that the weighing pan's cross axle rests on top of the catch-and-pin assembly inside, and cover the rest of the scale's top with smooth tiles.

# Kitchen scale

Use your bricks to make a scale that really reacts to the weights you place on its platform. Tech 4 discovers that when you're the size of a LEGO minifigure, this human tool makes a great trampoline!

## 1 ▶ Inner workings

When creating a model with a built-in function, start by thinking about how the parts of the mechanism will work together. LEGO Technic pieces threaded onto a cross axle will move together when the axle turns.

A strongly gripping bushing holds the gear in position

Push a LEGO Technic pin with a cross-axle end into a catch with cross hole

Note this 1x1 brick with handle built into the wall next to the gap—it's important!

## 2 ▶ Mechanism in place

Attach the mechanism's components to a base platform, like this 8x8 plate. Test the parts to make sure the cross axle rotates smoothly, and then start building up the scale's sides.

A 1x2 tile inside keeps the pin from getting stuck on the base's studs

The brick with hole fits into this gap in the front wall

## 3 ▶ Dial it up

To make the scale's dial, slide a short LEGO Technic cross axle through a 1x2 brick with a round hole. Connect a small half gear on one side, and a LEGO Technic tooth piece on the other.

Large round plate for a weighing pan

## 5 ▶ A scale model

Build a weighing pan by attaching a 2x2 round brick underneath a large plate. Push a cross axle into the hole in the center of the 2x2 brick, and thread its other end through a tile with a hole and a plate with holes. Push a half bushing onto the end of the axle so it won't pop back out.

The elastic band pulls the catch and pin upwards

## 4 ▶ Elastic power

To give your scale a springy resistance when its top is pushed down, take a LEGO elastic band and give it a twist in the middle. Loop one end over the handle of a brick with handle in the wall, and the other over the LEGO Technic catch and pin attached to the central cross axle.

Side walls keep the main axle from sliding back and forth

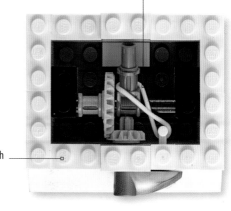

# Bathroom

Tech 4 finds himself inside a white, tiled chamber full of immense porcelain sculptures. Could this be the cavernous bathroom of some giant creature? What can you build from your own human bathroom?

Beak is an orange curved slope

Round 1x1 tile eyes attached to 1x1 bricks with side studs

Wings built around a 2x4 plate that sticks out on both sides of the body

FANCY A DIP?

## Rubber ducky

Quack! Quack! Get out your yellow bricks and build yourself a life-sized rubber ducky model. This bathtime favorite uses slope bricks and tiles to create its smooth, studs-free shape. Build the head first, then construct the body from the base up.

WHO'S THAT HANDSOME CHAP?

Build the reflection out of one-stud-wide bricks and tiles

THAT FACE LOOKS VERY FAMILIAR.

Drawer handles are LEGO Technic balls attached to 1x2 bricks with holes using LEGO Technic pins

## Shaving mirror

Who's that in the reflection of this tilting mirror? It's whoever you want it to be! Use your LEGO pieces mosaic-style to make up a funny face, or even build a bricky version of yourself.

LEGO Technic "friction" pin allows controlled rotation

1x1 brick with round hole

1x1 column

## Tilting function

The side supports for the mirror are built from tall and round elements. The tilting function comes from the LEGO Technic connector pins plugged into round holes in both the supports and the mirror frame.

Bristles made from 1x1
round bricks on a 2x6 plate

## Toothbrush

You could make a simple toothbrush
out of regular LEGO bricks, but this
one is a bit more stylish! Use 2x2
round elements for the handle, and
clip-and-bar hinges for an angled neck.

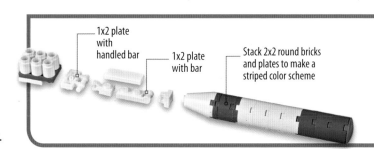

1x2 plate
with
handled bar

1x2 plate
with bar

Stack 2x2 round bricks
and plates to make a
striped color scheme

## Flexible neck

The neck of the toothbrush is made
by locking a plate with bar and
a plate with clip together with
a tile on top. They attach to a clip
on the handle and a bar on the head.

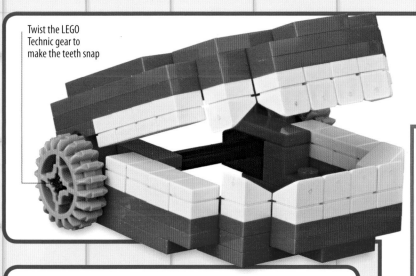

Twist the LEGO
Technic gear to
make the teeth snap

## Dentures

It looks like someone has left a set of false teeth on the sink…or is
this a pair of chattering joke teeth? Use tiles and 1x1 slopes to make a
mouthful of shiny white teeth, with a turning gear to make them move!

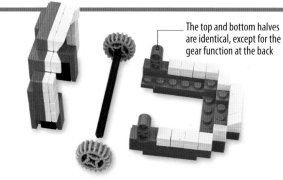

The top and bottom halves
are identical, except for the
gear function at the back

### Biting function

A LEGO Technic cross axle goes through pieces with round holes on the
lower jaw, and bricks with cross-shaped holes on the upper jaw.

## Comb

Use one-stud-wide pieces to build the flat handle of a comb. A row of
LEGO antennae makes a great line of long, thin teeth! With even more
antennae, you could use the same techniques to build a hairbrush, too.

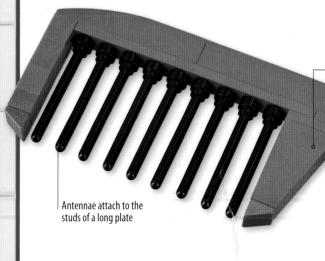

Stack up slopes and bricks to
make the handle extensions
around the teeth

Antennae attach to the
studs of a long plate

**A 1x6 inverted curved
slope holds the end of the
comb together.**

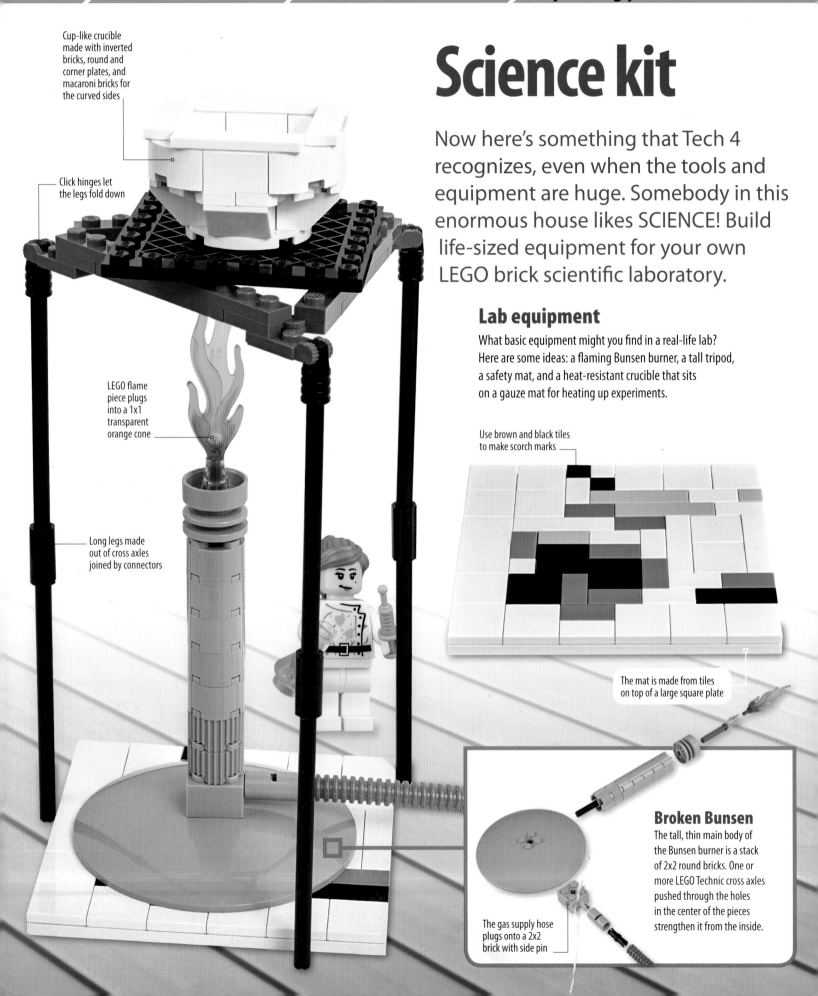

Cup-like crucible made with inverted bricks, round and corner plates, and macaroni bricks for the curved sides

Click hinges let the legs fold down

LEGO flame piece plugs into a 1x1 transparent orange cone

Long legs made out of cross axles joined by connectors

# Science kit

Now here's something that Tech 4 recognizes, even when the tools and equipment are huge. Somebody in this enormous house likes SCIENCE! Build life-sized equipment for your own LEGO brick scientific laboratory.

## Lab equipment

What basic equipment might you find in a real-life lab? Here are some ideas: a flaming Bunsen burner, a tall tripod, a safety mat, and a heat-resistant crucible that sits on a gauze mat for heating up experiments.

Use brown and black tiles to make scorch marks

The mat is made from tiles on top of a large square plate

### Broken Bunsen

The tall, thin main body of the Bunsen burner is a stack of 2x2 round bricks. One or more LEGO Technic cross axles pushed through the holes in the center of the pieces strengthen it from the inside.

The gas supply hose plugs onto a 2x2 brick with side pin

# Tongs

Handle your LEGO experiments with care by using a set of tongs to move your test tubes around the lab. Thanks to the clever use of a rubber band, this full-sized model works just like the real thing!

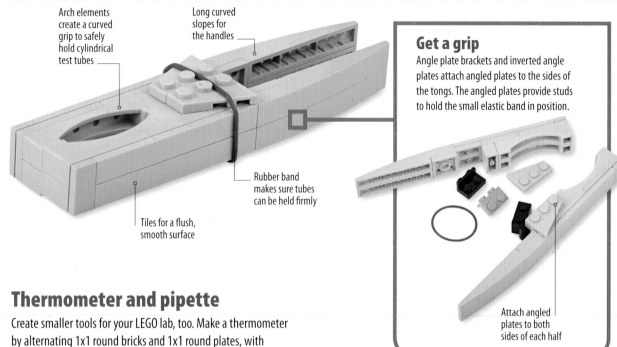

Arch elements create a curved grip to safely hold cylindrical test tubes

Long curved slopes for the handles

Rubber band makes sure tubes can be held firmly

Tiles for a flush, smooth surface

## Get a grip

Angle plate brackets and inverted angle plates attach angled plates to the sides of the tongs. The angled plates provide studs to hold the small elastic band in position.

Attach angled plates to both sides of each half

# Thermometer and pipette

Create smaller tools for your LEGO lab, too. Make a thermometer by alternating 1x1 round bricks and 1x1 round plates, with a LEGO Technic ball at the bottom. For a measuring pipette, plug a bar into a stack of 1x1 round bricks for the thin tip, and build a squeezing bulb with a 2x2 radar dish, cone, and dome.

A small LEGO Technic cross axle holds this cone and dome together

**PIPETTE**

**THERMOMETER**

Red pieces indicate temperature

# Test tubes

Build see-through test tubes out of clear round pieces, with colored elements for the mysterious chemicals bubbling and swirling inside. Make different colors and fluid levels for variety, and don't forget a rack to hold them upright!

Clear wheels for rims

Tubes are upside-down stacks of transparent 2x2 round bricks

This cross-axle connection lets the top and bottom ends of the stopper point in opposite directions

Replace a clear brick with a solid-colored one for the part of the stopper that's inside the tube

Use domes in matching colors for the bases

# Rubber stopper

The stopper's top is a stack of two 2x2 round plates and a round tile, attached to a LEGO Technic cross axle pushed through the center hole of the wheel rim.

**Try mixing different colors or adding detail pieces at the top to build chemical reactions into your tubes!**

# A banana

That was a close scrape! Tech 4 isn't sure what he just escaped from, but this looks like a much safer place to explore. In fact, it smells delicious…if a little over-ripe. Build life-sized food with your LEGO bricks, starting with a partly blackened banana!

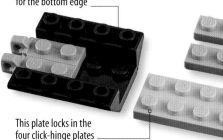

**START HERE**

This 4x4 sloped wedge piece provides the perfect curve for the bottom edge

This plate locks in the four click-hinge plates

## 1  Round the bend

Begin with one of the two middle sections of the banana. Because the model will be made up of jointed segments to give it a realistic curve, place click-hinge plates at both ends.

Use bricks for solid-color sections, or plates to make spots and patterns

## 2  Shades of ripeness

A perfectly ripe banana is all yellow, but this one may have gone off a bit! As you build up this body section with yellow bricks and plates, sprinkle in a few black ones to show age.

Angle the stem to follow the curve of the rest of the banana

The stem is a 2x2 cone, 1x1 round brick, and 1x1 slope, attached to the tip with a snap-together hinge

*AM I DREAMING?*

Left and right 2x4 angled plates

Click-hinge prong plates attach the top to the next body segment

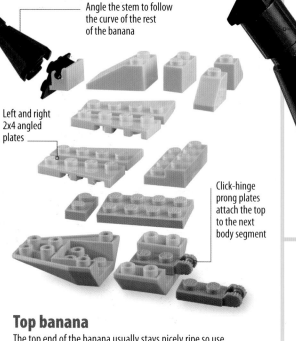

## Top banana

The top end of the banana usually stays nicely ripe so use mostly yellow bricks for it, plus some black pieces for the pointy tip where it was snapped off from the rest of the bunch. Underneath are inverted, sloped wedge pieces, while slopes and angled plates give it shape on top.

## 3 ▸ Finish the segment

Build the top of the banana segment with slope bricks, mirroring the shape of the angled piece underneath. Next, make another section with the same shape, but choose a different pattern of yellow and black pieces.

Use 2x2 or 1x2 slopes, depending on how big you want each block of color to be

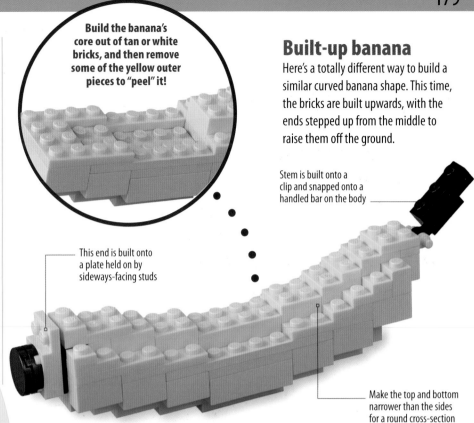

**Build the banana's core out of tan or white bricks, and then remove some of the yellow outer pieces to "peel" it!**

### Built-up banana

Here's a totally different way to build a similar curved banana shape. This time, the bricks are built upwards, with the ends stepped up from the middle to raise them off the ground.

Stem is built onto a clip and snapped onto a handled bar on the body

This end is built onto a plate held on by sideways-facing studs

Make the top and bottom narrower than the sides for a round cross-section

## 4 ▸ Creativity with a curve

Once you've made another body section, assemble the two ends too (see the breakdowns of those to find out how), then combine the pieces into one amazing banana! By placing the click hinges near the bottom of each segment, you can bend them just enough to make a curved shape.

The second section is closer to the all-black end, so it has more black pieces than the first one

2x4 left and right angled bricks build up the tapering sides

Include click-hinge tab plates to connect to the body

### Overripe tip

Large left-and right-side curved slopes on top mimic the shape of the inverted curved slope underneath this end of the banana. A LEGO Technic pin stuck into a 1x2 brick with hole attaches the round plate to the end.

# Fruit and veg

Tech 4's further investigation reveals an entire larder full of colossal produce, enough for a minifigure space colony to live off for years! After building a banana, what other fruits or vegetables could you make?

**WHAT'S NEXT**

Fruit and vegetables come in all shapes and sizes, so chances are you will have LEGO pieces in your collection that can make something delicious.

**APPLE**

**CHILI PEPPERS**

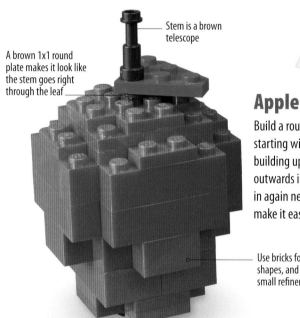

Stem is a brown telescope

A brown 1x1 round plate makes it look like the stem goes right through the leaf

## Apple

Build a round object like an apple by starting with a circle at the base and building up, stepping your bricks outwards in the center and then back in again near the top. A leaf and stem make it easy to identify this fruit!

Use bricks for big, blocky shapes, and plates for small refinements

A LEGO Technic cross axle connects the stem to the pepper top

1x2 slope

## Chili curve

Build a bend into your pepper model with a snap-together hinge that combines a 1x2 base and a 2x2 movable plate. A 1x2 slope fills in the gap between the two halves.

Most of this chili is made from 2x4 angled plates

1x2 plate and a 1x1 cone for the stem

A single-stud connection lets you attach the point at an angle

2x2 cone tip

## Chilis

Watch out—these chili peppers are red hot! The challenge in building them is creating the bend in the middle. Assemble a simple chili out of angled plates, or use round pieces and a hinge for a more three-dimensional version.

## PEAR

The stem is a 1x1 round brick and 1x1 slope attached to a 2x2 cone

A two-piece hinge makes the top crooked

### Pear

Here's another way to build a rounded fruit! Unlike the traditionally constructed apple, this pear is built outwards from a central core of side-stud bricks.

### Pairs for pears

Start with a core that alternates double plates between rows of four side-stud bricks. Stack plates to make the four-stud-wide front and back, and the two-stud-wide left and right sides.

Back-to-back 1x1 bricks with side studs point in opposite directions

Place two 2x2 plates between each row of four side-stud bricks

2x2 round plate at the bottom

Mix dark pieces with light ones for a mottled look

## MUSHROOMS

ALL MY PRODUCE IS FRESHLY BUILT.

### Mushrooms

There are lots of different ways to make mushrooms. Try using radar dishes or domes for the big round cap, and 1x1 round bricks or 2x2 round bricks for the narrower, cylinder-shaped stalk.

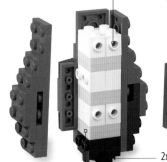

Textured round bricks add detail

Use a 2x2 dome for a smaller cap

Substitute colorful pieces for a toadstool, or gray and black for a cooked mushroom!

## CARROTS

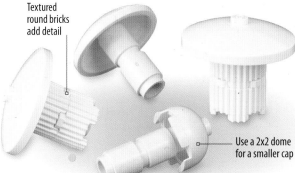

4x16 wedge slope body

The last round brick is flipped around and connected by a LEGO Technic cross-axle

### Carrots

If you've got orange and green LEGO elements, you can probably make a pretty good carrot! Here are two different ways to do it, one using lots of pieces and the other just a handful. How will you build yours?

### The root of it

Hold two long 4x16 wedges together by using short LEGO Technic cross-axles to attach pairs of 2x2 round plates back-to-back, so that the studs stick out on both sides. The carrot top attaches to a 1x2 jumper plate on two 1x1 headlight bricks.

Carrot body is a stack of 2x2 round bricks, with a 2x2 cone for the pointy end

# A gingerbread man

Tech 4 has discovered a new alien being!
Could this be the true ruling species of this
world, not those scary "human" creatures?
A gingerbread man is easier to build than
it is to bake. Here's how to do it!

**START HERE**

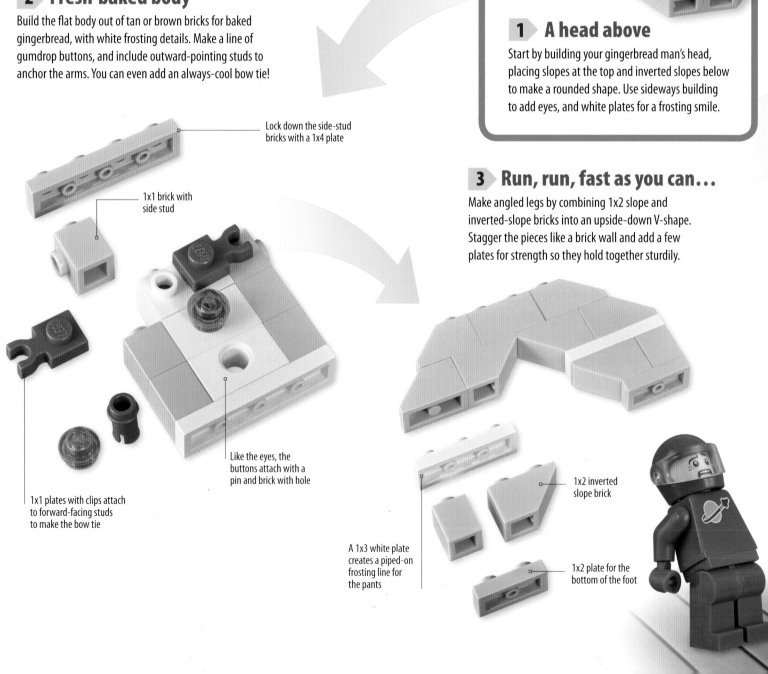

A 1x2 tile covers
the top studs

Eyes are printed 1x1
round tiles attached to
studded LEGO Technic
pins set in 1x2 bricks
with round holes

## 1   A head above

Start by building your gingerbread man's head,
placing slopes at the top and inverted slopes below
to make a rounded shape. Use sideways building
to add eyes, and white plates for a frosting smile.

## 2   Fresh-baked body

Build the flat body out of tan or brown bricks for baked
gingerbread, with white frosting details. Make a line of
gumdrop buttons, and include outward-pointing studs to
anchor the arms. You can even add an always-cool bow tie!

Lock down the side-stud
bricks with a 1x4 plate

1x1 brick with
side stud

Like the eyes, the
buttons attach with a
pin and brick with hole

1x1 plates with clips attach
to forward-facing studs
to make the bow tie

## 3   Run, run, fast as you can…

Make angled legs by combining 1x2 slope and
inverted-slope bricks into an upside-down V-shape.
Stagger the pieces like a brick wall and add a few
plates for strength so they hold together sturdily.

1x2 inverted
slope brick

A 1x3 white plate
creates a piped-on
frosting line for
the pants

1x2 plate for the
bottom of the foot

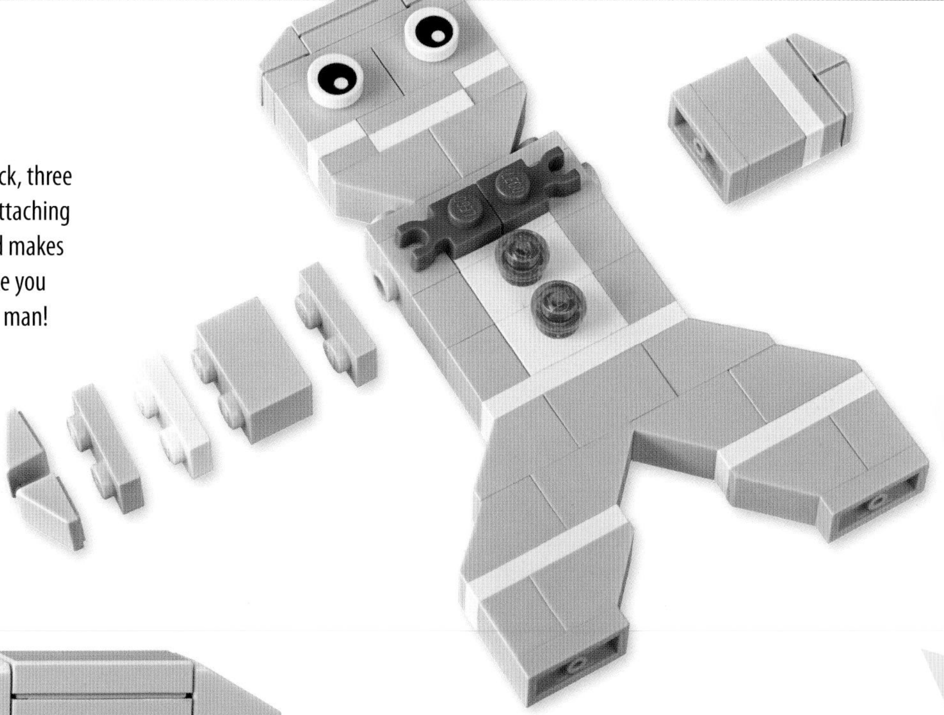

## 4 ▶ Pop-off arms

Each arm is made out of a 1x2 brick, three 1x2 plates, and two 1x1 slopes. Attaching them to the body by just one stud makes it easy to snap them off—just like you might do with a real gingerbread man!

**I'M ALIVE! I'M ALIVE!**

## 5 ▶ Ding! This batch is done

Your gingerbread man is complete! Now that you know how to build one, try making more gingerbread men and women with different designs of icing and candy decorations. Or you could just serve him up to your party guests...

**OH, CRUMBS.**

A transparent plate looks like a jelly candy

A frosting belt locks the bricks together at the base

Make crumbs with a few 1x1 round plates

**HALF-EATEN VIEW**

# More bakes

Deeper into the uncharted wilds of the pantry Tech 4 travels. There, hidden away inside of a gigantic jar labeled "Do Not Touch," he discovers a treasure trove that is almost as incredible…as it is edible!

**WHAT'S NEXT?**

You've already built one kind of dessert with your bricks. Now bake up a whole batch more! Try out these cookies and traybakes.

**CUSTARD CREAM**

## Custard cream

Build this sandwich cookie by assembling a pair of biscuits out of flat tan pieces, and using two white 2x2 jumper plates to make the custard-flavored filling in the middle.

Exposed studs mimic the traditional cookie's textured top

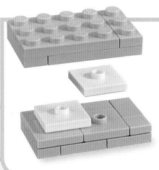

**Jumper layer**
The top layer of the bottom biscuit is covered with tiles and jumper plates so the filling pieces can sit in the center.

Upper biscuit made from two layers of plates

**COFFEE FUDGE BROWNIE**

Tiles for a smooth frosted top

## Coffee fudge brownie

Use plates of different shades of brown to make the fudge-filled brownie, and coat with a layer of tiles for coffee frosting.

Long and short plates lock the levels of the build together securely

For a different recipe, try nougat-colored pieces and make millionaire's shortbread!

*WE ALL GO VERY WELL WITH A CUP OF TEA.*

# CHOCOLATE BISCUIT

## Chocolate biscuit

This three-layered treat uses a simple combination of brown plates for the long chocolate biscuits, and dark brown plates for the chocolate buttercream filling squashed in between.

The order of the 1x6 and 2x6 plates alternates with each row

Since there aren't any 3x6 LEGO plates, you'll need to combine multiple six-stud-long pieces to get the right shape

# CHOCOLATE SANDWICH COOKIE

## Chocolate sandwich cookie

Two black 4x4 round plates are a perfect match for this snack's chocolate cookie top and bottom. A white 2x2 jumper plate in the center provides a single middle stud, so you can twist off the top part to get to the cream filling!

Hole connects to jumper plate's stud

### Cream filling

Place 1x2 tiles around the jumper plate to fill out this cookie's cream filling without blocking the twist-off function.

# COOKIES

## Cookies

Take four brown, tan, or nougat-colored corner plates and lock them together with a few plates on top to make chunky, lumpy homemade cookies. Pop on some 1x1 round plates or tiles for the chips!

Use multicolored pieces for rainbow chips, or black or brown for chocolate

Remove one or two plates for a bitten cookie

# Cakes and pastries

Look at the LEGO pieces in your collection to decide what baked goods to build. Round pieces could become a Bakewell tart, or square pieces a Battenberg cake. If you have angled plates and hinges, you could even build a festive slice of birthday cake!

**WHAT'S NEXT?**

After trying out some flatter cookies and traybakes, try building up a batch of cakes. Use these sweet ideas to inspire you.

## Lemon slice

Put together plates to make a rectangle of lemon-flavored cake with a sweet cream filling, and use yellow jumper plates to attach white tiles for diagonal stripes of frosting on top.

**LEMON SLICE**

Tiles on top hide the breaks between three yellow 1x2 jumper plates

The 1x3 tiles that form the frosting stripes are attached at an angle on the single studs of jumper plates.

Yellow 1x6 tiles for the outer edges

**BATTENBERG CAKE**

Studded surfaces give the cake a sugary texture

Each side is a 4x8 tan plate

## Battenberg cake

Start this distinctively decorative cake by using yellow and pink tiles to build a checkered pattern on two 4x4 plates at the ends. A core covered with sideways-studded brackets lets you build the sides by attaching plates that face outwards in all directions.

If you don't have enough brackets to go inside the cake, you could build up the center as a stack of bricks instead.

# CHERRY BAKEWELLS

This tart uses the same pieces for its top as the brick-built one

## Cherry Bakewells

To build a tasty tart, start with a round, brown base—you could construct it from bricks, or use a large half barrel to keep it simple. Add a layer or two of white pieces for the almond fondant, and attach a red LEGO Technic ball to the top for a candied cherry.

1x2 slopes for sloping edges

### The secret ingredient

A 4x4 radar dish fits on top of a half-barrel

Inside the half-barrel, a 2x2 round brick with a LEGO Technic cross axle pushed through its center hole forms a support column for a round radar dish.

Shortcrust pastry shell built from tan bricks and plates

# BIRTHDAY CAKE

Plug in a flame piece at the top

Flower element for a candle-holder

## Birthday cake

To make a slice of cake, arrange angled plates into a triangle for the frosted top, and then build a matching triangular base using hinged plates. Build up the sides and back, and attach the top portion. Add colorful decorations and don't forget a candle!

Use 1x1 plates with clips and rings for fancy frosting details

A white wall at the back for the cake's frosted edge

Make jelly-like layers of fruit filling with transparent colored round and square plates

Include multiple hinge plates for strength

Try different color bricks for different cake flavors, such as yellow for vanilla or brown for chocolate

## Have a slice

Try narrow hinged plates at the tip of your cake slice, and wide-open ones at the back. The sides of the cake are constructed like brick walls, with layers of filling and frosting inside.

*I THINK ONE SLICE WILL BE ENOUGH.*

# A popsicle

Tech 4 has found a portal to an ice region. Behind this heavy door is a labyrinth of frozen food. Cautiously, he unwraps something shaped like a spaceship and takes a bite. It's a delicious three-color popsicle!

START
HERE

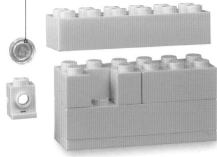

Transparent 1x1 round tile for ice—you could also use a round plate, or a colored piece for melting fruit juice

### 1 > An ice beginning

Start building your popsicle with the 2x6 bottom layer, its widest section. Bricks with side studs let you attach transparent pieces as tiny chunks of ice.

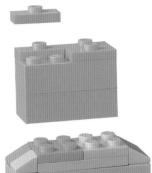

### 2 > Onward and upward

Next, switch colors and build the 2x4 middle section of the popsicle as a smaller wall of bricks, using slopes for an angled transition from the larger section beneath it. Place four 1x2 jumper plates at the top.

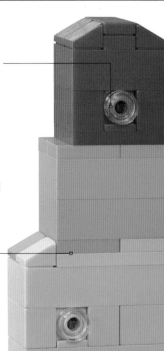

Recessed 1x1 headlight bricks make the ice sit close to the surface

### 4 > A cool creation

Add a lollipop-style stick at the bottom, and your popsicle is complete! Try building the same design with different colors and patterns of melting ice. You could even make a patriotic version in the colors of a flag!

The colors of a real popsicle melt into each other, so mix in a few pieces in the middle section

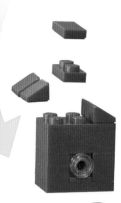

### 3 > Tasty top

Change colors again for the 2x3 top section. The offset studs of the jumper plates underneath will center it on the middle section. Use 1x1 slopes and a 1x2 plate and tile to give it a rounded tip.

*I HOPE THESE ARE AS COOL AS MY TUNES.*

### Stick-y situation

The popsicle stick is made by connecting three white cylinder-shaped LEGO Technic connectors together with black LEGO® Technic connector pins. A pin with a cross-axle end at the top fits into the popsicle's base.

# Frozen treats

What other desserts from the freezer can you make? With the right shapes and colors, you can combine your LEGO bricks to construct tall or flat ice-lollies, and even chocolate-covered ice-cream bars.

**WHAT'S NEXT?** Some of the same techniques used to make a popsicle can be used for other kinds of frozen snacks, too.

*SWIRLY SURPRISE*

*CHOCO BITE*

*STRAWBERRY DIP*

1x2 tiles and a 2x2 radar dish attached to a 2x2 jumper plate on top

Leave off some brown pieces and add white slopes to make it look like someone has taken a bite!

Stack tan 1x2 bricks for a wooden popsicle stick

Attach 1x1 round plates to bricks with side studs for candy bits

## Swirly surprise

Try a chilly challenge with the more complicated shape of a striped ice lolly. Make a cross-shaped stack of 2x4 bricks using two different colors. Alternate the colours in each stack to make stripes.

## Choco bite

Build a simple chocolate ice cream bar by building a brick wall with slopes at the top. The rows of this one have alternating pairs of 2x2 and 2x3 bricks for strength.

## Strawberry dip

Change up the colors and details on a simple ice cream bar for variety. This one has a top in a different color for a "dipped" look.

# Candy gallery

When you're building life-sized sweets, the whole world is your candy barrel. Use clear pieces for wrappers, cross axles and antenna pieces for sticks, and all the colors of the LEGO brick rainbow!

**LIQUORICE STACKS**

**LIQUORICE TUBE**

**SUNSHINE SWEET**

**TOFFEE DROP**

**LIME ZING**

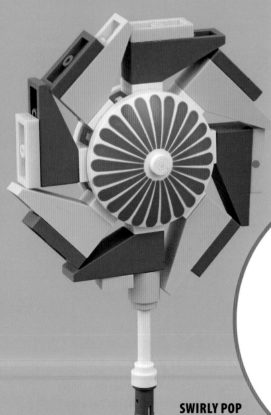

**SWIRLY POP**

**CANDY CANE**

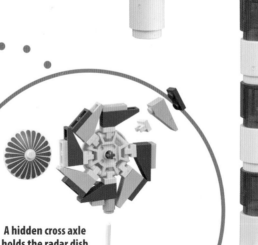

A hidden cross axle holds the radar dish center of this lollipop in place. It fits through an octagonal plate with bars.

**SAUCER POP**

**LIQUORICE STACKS**

**BERRY BITE**

**BLUE BULLET**

**LEMON SWIRL**

**ALPINE MINT**

A LEGO Technic cross axle holds the back-to-back plates in place.

**BUTTERMINT**

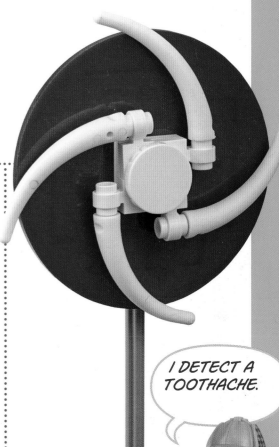

*I DETECT A TOOTHACHE.*

**TROPICAL POP**

**STRAWBERRY POP**

**BLUEBERRY POP**

**PINWHEEL POP**

Use plates and tiles to build the ribbon

Curved half-arch pieces form a box-top bow

Gift note made from two angled plates

### Room for dessert
The box's lining is built from black bricks and covered with smooth tiles. Tiles at the bottom of each compartment make the chocolates easy to remove.

### Chocolate box
Once you've built up your chocolate treats, build compartments that are the perfect fit for them. Once you're done, build a box for them all with a removable lid. You could also add a bow and a gift note to the box to make it look extra fancy.

The box is built on a big 16x16 plate, but you could combine several smaller ones

# Box of chocolates

Tech 4 has received a reply from his starship. Help is on the way! There's just enough time to explore one last find: a box full of fancy chocolates, each one tantalizingly unique. Tech 4 needs to taste…erm…test them all!

## Chocolate selection

When designing chocolates, don't just use plain brown bricks. Add tan pieces for nutty toppings, white for white chocolate details, and don't forget that one special gold-wrapped morsel.

Sideways stack of brown and black plates with a tile on top

Hazelnut cap made from a sliding plate on a 3x3 hemisphere.

Grilles for thin white chocolate stripes

Tooth plate attached to a jumper plate stud

Gold-wrapped chocolate made with a 2x2 dome, four 1x1 round plates, and a 2x2 round plate.

Flower plate for a decorative topping

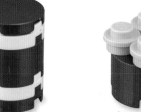

1x1 round plates make a chopped nut topping

Horn elements attach to 1x1 plates with top clips.

Tech 4 still isn't at home in the real world.

# Brick gallery

There are thousands of LEGO® pieces used in the models in this book. Here are a few useful pieces you might have in your own collection. They are all waiting for you to start creating your own LEGO world.

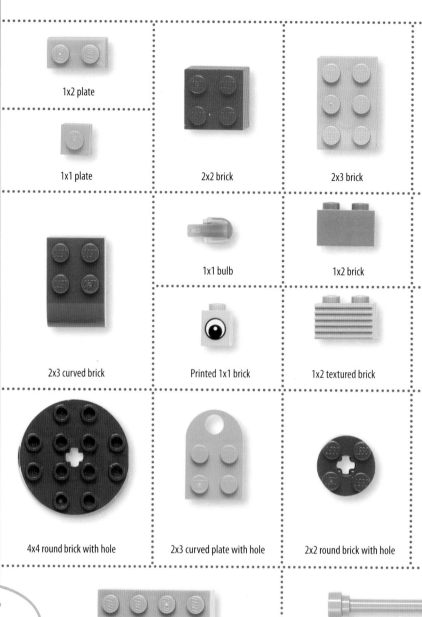

1x2 plate

1x1 plate

2x2 brick

2x3 brick

1x1x5 brick

2x3 curved brick

1x1 bulb

1x2 brick

1x3 curved slope

Printed 1x1 brick

1x2 textured brick

1x1 round brick

4x4 round brick with hole

2x3 curved plate with hole

2x2 round brick with hole

1x2 brick with 2 holes

1x4 plate

Antenna

LEGO® Technic axle

Bar

Robot arm

4x6 plate

2x2 turntable

Headlight brick

RIGHT, I NEED SOME 1X2 BRICKS, TWO HINGE PLATES, AND A BAR.

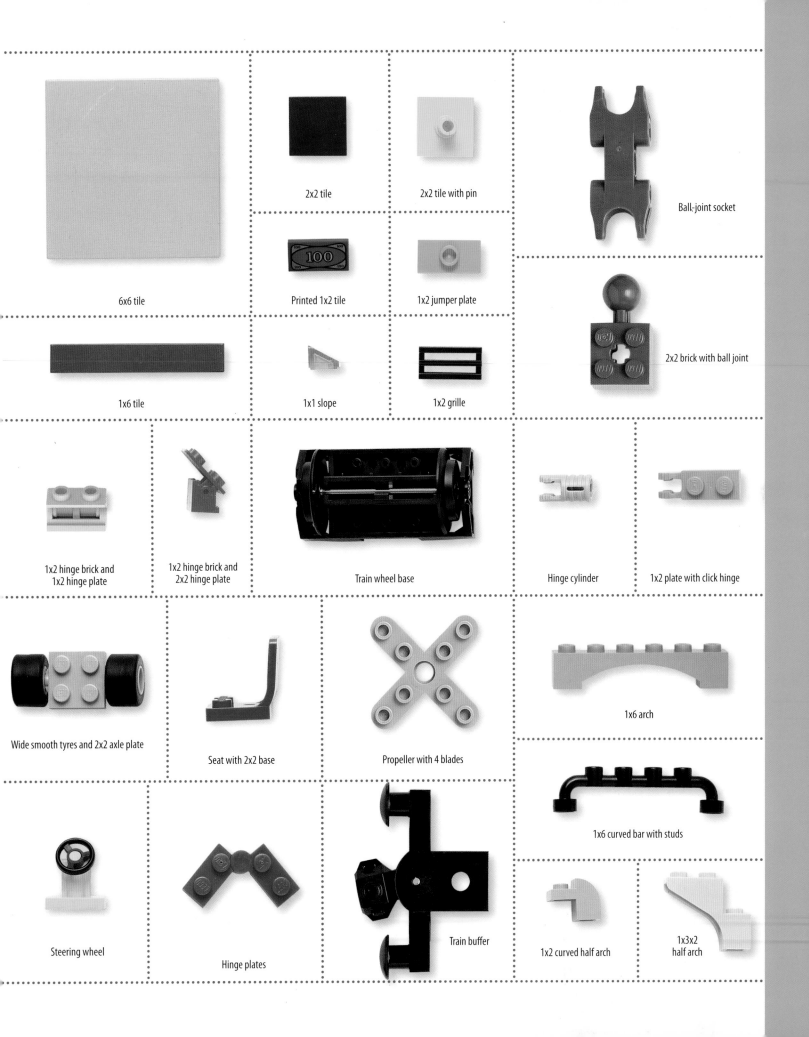

6x6 tile

2x2 tile

2x2 tile with pin

Ball-joint socket

Printed 1x2 tile

1x2 jumper plate

2x2 brick with ball joint

1x6 tile

1x1 slope

1x2 grille

1x2 hinge brick and
1x2 hinge plate

1x2 hinge brick and
2x2 hinge plate

Train wheel base

Hinge cylinder

1x2 plate with click hinge

Wide smooth tyres and 2x2 axle plate

Seat with 2x2 base

Propeller with 4 blades

1x6 arch

1x6 curved bar with studs

Steering wheel

Hinge plates

Train buffer

1x2 curved half arch

1x3x2
half arch

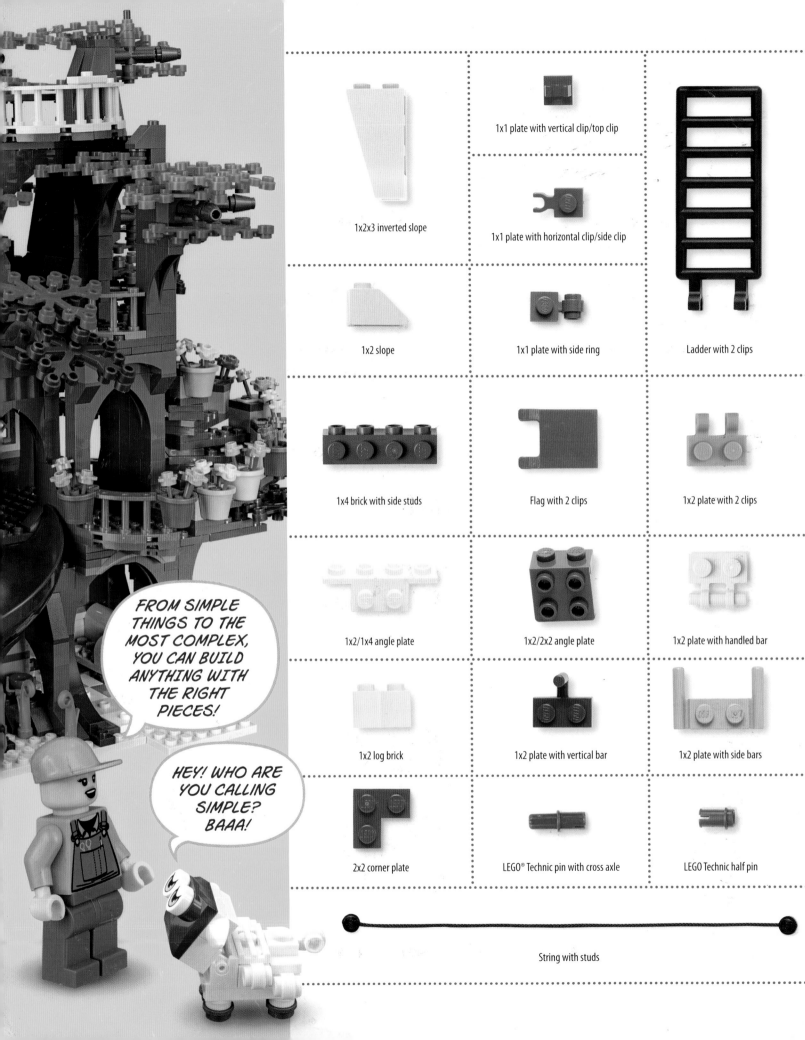

1x2x3 inverted slope

1x1 plate with vertical clip/top clip

1x1 plate with horizontal clip/side clip

Ladder with 2 clips

1x2 slope

1x1 plate with side ring

1x4 brick with side studs

Flag with 2 clips

1x2 plate with 2 clips

1x2/1x4 angle plate

1x2/2x2 angle plate

1x2 plate with handled bar

1x2 log brick

1x2 plate with vertical bar

1x2 plate with side bars

2x2 corner plate

LEGO® Technic pin with cross axle

LEGO Technic half pin

String with studs

FROM SIMPLE THINGS TO THE MOST COMPLEX, YOU CAN BUILD ANYTHING WITH THE RIGHT PIECES!

HEY! WHO ARE YOU CALLING SIMPLE? BAAA!

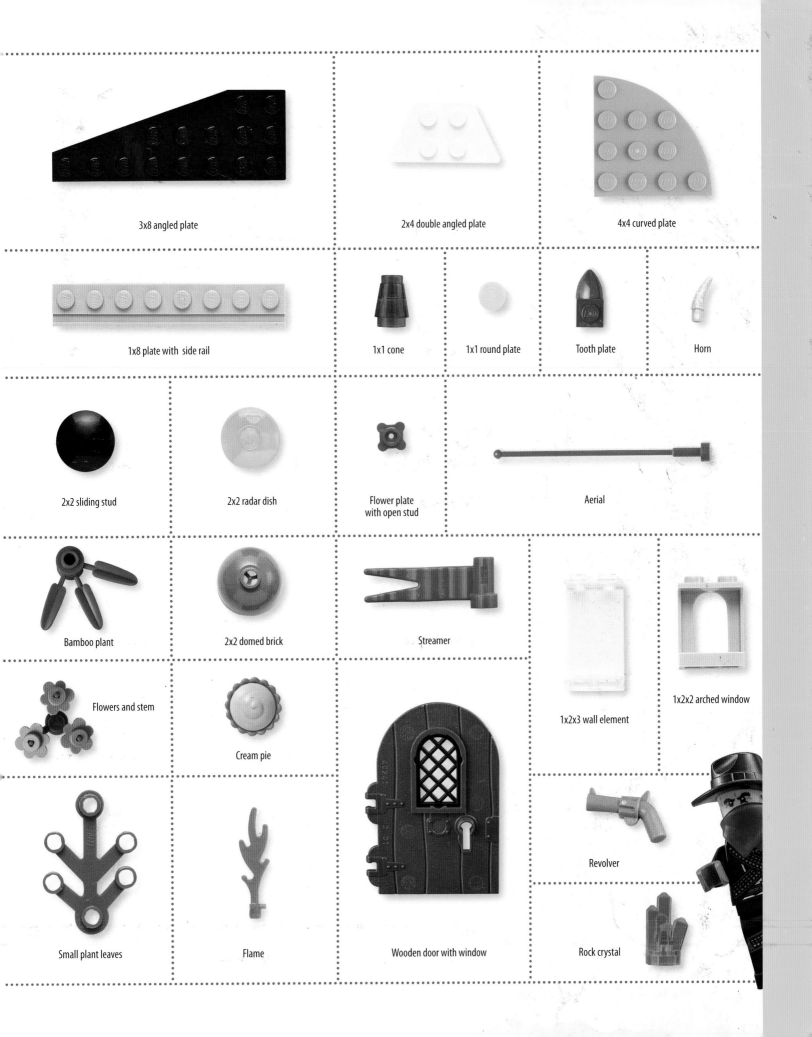

3x8 angled plate

2x4 double angled plate

4x4 curved plate

1x8 plate with side rail

1x1 cone

1x1 round plate

Tooth plate

Horn

2x2 sliding stud

2x2 radar dish

Flower plate with open stud

Aerial

Bamboo plant

2x2 domed brick

Streamer

1x2x3 wall element

1x2x2 arched window

Flowers and stem

Cream pie

Small plant leaves

Flame

Wooden door with window

Revolver

Rock crystal

Penguin Random House

**Senior Editor** Hannah Dolan
**Senior Designer** Lisa Sodeau
**Project Art Editor** Lauren Adams
**Design Assistant** Ellie Bilbow
**Pre-Production Producer** Siu Chan
**Senior Producer** Louise Daly
**Managing Editor** Simon Hugo
**Design Manager** Guy Harvey
**Art Director** Lisa Lanzarini
**Publisher** Julie Ferris
**Publishing Director** Simon Beecroft

Models built by Yvonne Doyle, Alice Finch, Rod Gillies, Tim Goddard,
Tim Johnson, Barney Main, Drew Maughan, and Pete Reid
Photography by Gary Ombler
Cover design by Jon Hall

Dorling Kindersley would like to thank Randi Sørensen, Henk van der Does,
Melody Caddick, Alexandra Martin, Heike Bornhausen, Paul Hansford, Robert Ekblom,
and Lisbeth Finnemann Skrumsager at the LEGO Group. Thanks also to Pamela Afram,
Beth Davies, Andy Jones, Matt Jones, and Scarlett O'Hara at DK for editorial assistance,
and Jon Hall, Pamela Shiels, Rhys Thomas, and Jade Wheaton for design assistance.

First American Edition, 2015
Published in the United States by DK Publishing
345 Hudson Street, New York, New York 10014

DK books are available at special discounts when purchased in bulk for
sales promotions, premiums, fund-raising, or educational use. For details, contact:
DK Publishing Special Markets, 345 Hudson Street, New York, New York 10014
SpecialSales@dk.com

A CIP catalog record for this book is available from the Library of Congress.

ISBN: 978-1-4654-3788-4

Color reproduction by Tranistics Data Technologies Pvt. Ltd.
Printed in China

www.LEGO.com
www.dk.com

A WORLD OF IDEAS:
**SEE ALL THERE IS TO KNOW**